Islam in China

Written by Mi Shoujiang & You Jia
Translated by Min Chang

CHINA INTERCONTINENTAL PRESS

TABLE OF CONTENTS

Chapter 5. Chinese Islam in New Times

PREFACE

As early as in the middle of the 7th century, Islam was introduced into China. Having spread and developed for 1300 years, going through the Tang, Song, Yuan, Ming and Qing dynasties and the Republic Period (618-1949 A.D.), Islam has developed more than 20 million followers (Muslims) in China. It was called by different names in different historic periods. In the Tang Dynasty (618-907 A.D.), Islam was called "Dashi Jiao" (religion of Dashi. Arabs were called Dashi then); in the Ming Dynasty (1368-1644 A.D.), it was called "Tianfang Jiao" (religion of Arabia), or "Hui Hui Jiao" (religion of the Hui Huis. Muslims of various ethnic backgrounds were generally called Hui Hui then); at the end of the Ming Dynasty and the beginning of the Qing Dynasty (1616-1911 A.D.), it was called "Qingzhen Jiao" (pure and true religion); in the Republic Period (1912-1949 A.D.), it was called "Hui Jiao" (religion of the Huis, which is a Muslim ethnic group in China). After New China was founded in 1949, the State Council issued "Notice Concerning the Name of Islam" in 1956, pointing out: "Islam is an internationalized religion, and the term of 'Islam' is the internationally used common name for this religion." "Do not use the term of 'Hui Jiao' for Islam henceforth, simply call it Islam." Since then, the term of Islam was commonly used on the mainland of China, while it was still called "Hui Jiao" in Hong Kong, Macao and Taiwan. Among the 56 ethnic groups in China, there are 10, namely the Huis, the Uighurs, the Kazaks, the Dongxiangs, the Khalkhas, the Salas, the Tajiks, the Uzbeks, the Bao'ans and the Tatars, that take Islam as their national faith. There are a small number of Muslims among the Mongolians, the Tibetans, the Bais and the Dais as well.

Islam exerted great influence on the social life of China, especially on the social development and ethnic traditions of the 10 minority groups that take Islam as their national faith. Muslims in China have and are still making great contributions to the development of politics, the economy, and the culture of China as well.

Chapter 1
Spread and Development of Islam in China

1. Advent of Islam to China

It remains an open question when Islam was first introduced into China. For a long period of time, many scholars have been working on this matter, and reached different conclusions. A popular theory advanced by well-known contemporary historian Chen Yuan indicates that it was in the second year of Yonghui of the Tang Dynasty (651 A.D.). He found out actual records in "History of Tang" and "Cefu Yuangui (Guide to Books)": In the second year of Yonghui of Emperor Gaozong of Tang, the third Caliph of Arabia Othman (on the throne in 644-656 A.D.)

dispatched diplomatic envoys to Chang'an, capital city of Tang, to pay an official call to Emperor Gaozong, introducing to him the caliphate, their customs and Islam. For historic purposes most of scholars have acknowledged this year as the symbol of Islam's advent into China.

It is through two routes that Islam was introduced into China: the Sea Route and the Land Route. Since Zhangqian (?-114 A.D.) was sent as an envoy to the Western Region (A Han Dynasty term for the area including now Xinjiang and Central Asia) in the Han Dynasty, the transportation and communication between China and the countries to the west had started. In the 9th year of Yongyuan of Emperor Hanhe of the Han Dynasty, Ganying reached the Arabian Peninsula in person when he was sent on a diplomatic mission to the Western Region. In the Tang Dynasty, the transportation and communication between China and the west was further developed. The Land Road starting from Southwest Asia, via Persia, Afghanistan, Central Asia, the Tianshan Mountains and Hexi Corridor, to Chang'an, capital of Tang, was an important passage linking China and the west. A great number of Muslim traders made long and arduous journeys into China to do business. In accordance with "Zi Zhi Tong Jian" (History as a Mirror), there were over 4000 foreign business in

Chang'an in the Tang Dynasty, among which the majority were Arabs and Persians, and the Tang government had to set up a "Trading Department" to be in charge of administration. The Tang Dynasty also had frequent military contacts with the Arab Islamic Empire. In 148 years' period of time from the second year of Yonghui of Emperor Gaozong (651 A.D.) to the 14th year of Zhenyuan of Emperor Dezong (798 A.D.), the recorded Arab envoys' visits to China reached 37. In the middle of the Tang Dynasty, the central authority was weakened by political corruption and social problems and the governors in control of outlying prefectures grew stronger. In the winter of 755 A.D., governor An Lushan, who was in control of Pingzhan, Fanyang and Hedong, rebelled in Fanyang (now Beijing), and Shi Shiming, a general under his control, captured a great part of Hebei in the mean time. This is an event historically called "Rebellion of An and Shi", which lasted 7 years and was eventually put down by the Tang government. From then on, the Tang regime became weaker and weaker. To put down "Rebellion of An and Shi", the Tang government asked for military help from the Arab Empire. Emperor Zongyun allowed the Arab soldiers to live in China permanently when the rebellion was over. As a result, Islam was introduced into the Northwest of China by Arab and Persian traders, diplomatic envoys and soldiers.

In the Tang Dynasty, Chinese and Arab traders dominated the sea business passage starting from Persian Gulf and Arab Sea, via the Gulf of Bangladesh, the Straits of Malacca and the South China Sea, to Chinese ports like Guangzhou, Quanzhou and Yangzhou. A great number of Arab and Persian traders come to these places to do business, and some of them settled down there. Thus, Islam was introduced into China by sea business.

The Tang and Song dynasties (618-1279 A.D.) were the first periods of Islam in China. Muslims in China at that time were basically composed of traders, soldiers and diplomatic envoys from Arabia, Persia and other countries. They settled down and lived in compact communities when they came to China, keeping their religion and unique way of life. The purpose they came to China was to do business rather than missionary work, therefore, they were not opposed by the Chinese ruling class, and were allowed to settle down and intermarry with local Chinese people. The Muslims who had taken up permanent residence in China were called Zhu Tang (literally means foreigners living China). These Zhu Tangs married local Chinese women and multiplied, and their descendants became native-born Fan Ke (meaning foreigner, actually referring to foreign

Muslims). However, Muslims at that time were of small number, concentrating in big cities and ports located along vital communication lines. Due to religious needs and national customs, they built mosques and lived in compact communities with the mosques as center. Today's mosques like the Huaisheng Mosque in Guangzhou (constructed in the Tang Dynasty), the Qingjing Mosque in Quanzhou (Masjid al-Ashab, translated as Shengyou Mosque, constructed in the Northern Song Dynasty), the Xianhe Mosque in Yangzhou (constructed in the Southern Song Dynasty) and the Fenghuang Mosque in Hangzhou

◎ Grand Mosque of Aksu, Xinjiang.

◎ Huaisheng Mosque in Guangzhou (constructed in the Tang Dynasty).

(constructed in the Yuan Dynasty) are called The Four Ancient Mosques in China.

During Tang and Song dynasties, as foreign trade developed, more Arab and Persian traders settled down in China. In the 4th year of Zhenghe of Song, there appeared the 5th generation of local-born Fan Ke. The Song government specially issued "Heritage Law for the 5th Generation of Local-born Fan Ke" to deal with their heritage matters. To adapt themselves to local society, the native-born Muslims in the Song Dynasty began to receive Chinese cultural education positively. In Guangzhou and Quanzhou where Muslims were concentrated, there appeared special schools run by Muslims themselves--Fan Xue (school for foreigners), which only or mainly recruited native-born Muslims' children. To set up Fan Xue, the local government had to apply to the courts for ratification. The purpose of building Fan Xue was to educate Muslim children with traditional Chinese culture and help them to adapt themselves to the society as soon as possible. The final target of Fan Xue was the imperial examination held by the court, which was the most important way to participate in politics. The Song Dynasty followed the Tang's system of allowing foreigners and their offspring living China to take the imperial examination with the same subjects as native Chinese examinees. Though the imperial examination system for them was not mature yet, the year's quota enabled the outstanding ones to directly engage in politics.

The intermarriage between foreign Muslims living in China and native Chinese became a common phenomenon. Among the first generation of foreign Muslims in China, most came alone. They were wealthy and enjoyed high social status, so intermarriage was not a difficult thing for them at all. They married girls from ordinary, official even royal families as well. Of course, there were some Muslim girls marrying Non-Muslims, but it would never happen unless they converted to Islam, because Islam requires that Non-Muslims, whether men or women, must all embrace Islam when they marry Muslims. As a result, the Muslim population in China increased.

Keeping slaves was another important way to increase the Muslim population. In the Song Dynasty, land annexation prevailed; some of the tenant-peasants who had lost their land sought refuge in official or rich families in order to change their identity or social status, or to escape certain social obligations, and became slaves. It was also a common phenomenon that some of the tenant-peasants sought refuge in Muslim families and embraced Islam at the same time. Keeping slaves was a natural thing for Muslims, because according to Islamic traditions, slaves of this sort were qualified to inherit part, even total estates of the master.

In a word, Muslims in the Song Dynasty became involved in all walks of social life by various means such as running schools, taking imperial examinations, inter-marrying and keeping slaves; resulting in the increase of the Muslim population and leading to the birth of a new ethnic group: the Huis.

The spread of Islam from China's western frontier was connected with the history of the Karakitai Dynasty. After the Tang Dynasty came to an end in 840 A.D., the Hui Hus (an ancient tribe believing in Islam) migrated to the west. One group of Hui Hus led by Pangteqin went westwards to the Chu River where the Garluq tribe was in occupation. Pangteqin and his clansmen submitted to Garluq and other Hui Hu tribes later, and built up a new Hui Hu regime which was historically called Karakitai. From the middle of the 9th century to the early 13th century, Karakitai lasted over 370 years. During the same period of time, the central region of China experienced an alternation of several dynasties from the Tang, to the Five Dynasties and Ten Kingdoms, to the Northern Song and the Southern Song (7th century to 13th century) dynasties. And at the same time in the north and northwest of China there appeared several other minority groups' regimes: the Western Liao, Jin and Western Xia.

In the early days, the Karakitai Dynasty practiced the double-Khan ruling system. The empire was divided into east and west branches for the elder and the younger sons of Khan. The east branch was under the rule of the elder brother who was chief khan and was known as Arslan Khan (king of lions). The capital of the east branch was located in Barashagon (now Tokmak, Kirghizstan). The west branch was ruled by the younger brother who was vice khan and was known as Boghra Khan (king of male camels). The capital of the west branch was located in Talas (now Dzhambul, Kazakstan). Satuk Boghra Khan, who was the primogenitor of the west branch, was the first khan of the Karakitai Dynasty to embrace Islam, whose Muslim name was

<p>
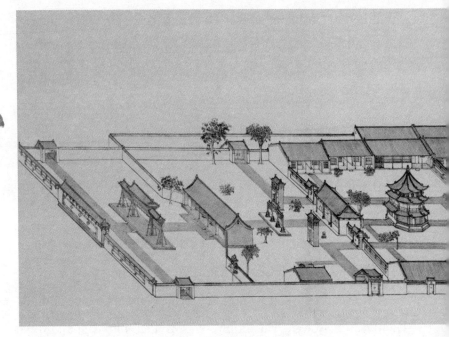

◎ The plain figure of the Huajuexiang Mosque in Xi'an, painted by a Muslim artist in the Ming Dynasty (1368-1398 A.D.).

Abdal Karim. It is said that Satuk was influenced by the Muslims of the Samanid Dynasty since his childhood, and eventually became a Muslim himself. Having seized power from his uncle by force, Satuk soon established Islamic rule as Arabian countries had done. He was on the throne for 45 years and died in 344 A.H. (955-956 A.D.). The Khanate became Islamic when his son Musa succeeded to the throne. In about 960 A.D, Musa declared Islam as the state religion, and 200 thousand Turk

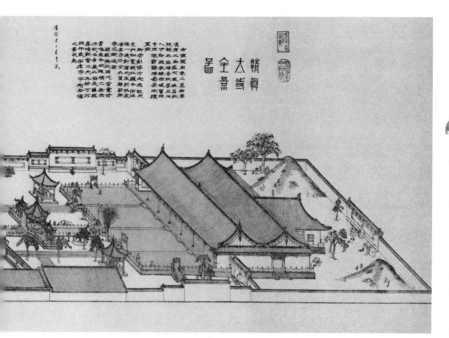

families were converted into Islam. Karakitai was the first minority's regime to take Islam as its state religion in Chinese history.

The Karakitai Dynasty became stronger since it had become Islamic. It conquered Yutian (now Hetian, Xinjiang), and its influence extended to Qiemo and Ruoqiang.

The rulers of Karakitai were extremely pious to Islam and did their best to implement Islamic ruling. Everywhere in the dynasty, Islamic courts were set up, and mosques and Islamic academies were established to foster capable personnel for

Islamic causes. Furthermore, a good number of famous Mazars (Arabic transliteration, originally meaning shrine or tombs of saints; here refers to the mausoleums of Muslim high officials) were constructed. In this period of time, large numbers of Turk nomads started to settle down, this helped to accelerate the transformation of the aborigines in the Central Asia into Turks and the Islamization of the nomads. The social economy and sciences further developed and Uighur Islamic culture took shape as a result. Outstanding works such as "Wisdom of Happiness", "Turk Dictionary" and "Basic Knowledge of Truth" are of a good reflection of this.

2.Extensive Spread of Islam in China

Since 1219, Genghis Khan (1162-1227 A.D.) with his sons and grandsons marched westwards three times and conquered Central Asia and China, and built up a huge empire spanning the European and Asian continents, including large Muslim areas. In the Kublai Khan's war against the Southern Song Dynasty to reunify China, many Arabs, Persians and Central Asians who believed in Islam organized the Western Region Army and participated in this war. When the war was over, these Muslim soldiers stayed where they fought to grow crops and graze horses. They were scattered all over the country, while many more were in the Northwest and a small number were dispersed in the Southwest and Central regions, afterwards some were moved south of the Yangtze River. Most of the Muslim soldiers coming along with the army usually did not take their families. They married local women and multiplied after they settled down. Moreover, the Mongols dispatched a great number of Muslim craftsmen to many places in the country, most of whom settled down where they worked. In the Yuan Dynasty, the Muslims from the Western Region and their descendants were called Hui Hui, who belonged to Se Mu (one of the four classes into which China's population was divided in the Yuan Dynasty, including Central Asian allies of the Mongols, mostly Uighurs and other Turks.). As Muslims in the Yuan Dynasty had made great contributions to the establishment of the Dynasty, they were given high social status that was only below that of the Mongols and above that of the Hans and the Southerners. The upper circle of Muslims were placed in important positions by Yuan rulers, and some of them ranked among the ruling class. In this period of time, the Muslim population increased at a sharp rate, and Islam spread and developed rapidly. The distribution structure of the Muslim population which could be described as "being dispersed widely and concentrated in small groups" was taking shape. It was a time when Islam experienced great development.

The development of Islam in the Yuan Dynasty was related to the birth and growth of the Hui Huis. The term "Hui Hui" appeared earliest in Shen Kuo's book "Meng Xi Bi Tan"(Notes Written in Dream) in the Northern Song Dynasty (960-1127 A.D.), referring to the Hui Hus in the Tang Dynasty. During the Tang and Song Dynasties, the Hui Hui had not come into being as an ethnic group, so it had nothing to do with Islamic religion. Since the Southern Song Dynasty (1127-1279 A.D.), the conception of the term of Hui Hui was broadened to cover the Muslim peoples, states and places in the Western Region. In the Yuan Dynasty, as the transportation and communication between China and the West further developed, large numbers of Muslims in West and Central Asia came to China. By then the term 'Hui Hui' referred to all Muslim groups immigrating from the Central Asia, Persia and Arabia to China. In the early period of the Yuan Dynasty, Muslims coming from the Sea Route were called "Nan Fan Hui Hui" (Muslims in the South). It was said in "Gui Xin Za Shi" by Zhou Mi: "Today, all the Hui Huis take the Central Region of China as their home, while there are many more in the south of the Yangtze River." By the second year of Emperor Xianzong (1252 A.D.), the term 'Hui Hui' was used in official census, and it became the special ethnic name of the Muslims living the central region of China in the Yuan Dynasty.

It was a long historic course that the Hui Huis were turned into an ethnic group. During the period of the Tang and Song Dynasties, the Arab and Persian Muslims who had already taken up permanent residence in China lived in commercial cities located on main traffic lines. They intermarried with local peoples and multiplied, and the population of the local-born Muslims increased steadily. They became the earliest Muslims in China and the ancestors of the Hui Huis.

The Mongols' three conquering marches to the west during the Yuan Dynasty (1206-1368 A.D.) led to the migration of various ethnic groups, classes and professionals to the east. They were not only confined to the cities located on traffic lines, but widely spread throughout the countryside, commercial towns and places where Chi Ma Tan Jun (Muslim troop composed of the tribes in the Western Region) stationed, covering a vast area from Mobei and Dadu (now Beijing) to the south of the Yangtze River, and Yuannan and the Northwest. The population and extension of the Hui Huis went far beyond that in the period of the Tang and Song Dynasties. They were allowed to marry local women and multiply when they settled down in various places, and as a result the population the Hui Huis increased at a sharp rate.

The Mongols' conquering marches to the west put an end to the splitting-up situation of the northern and southern sides of the Tianshan Mountains and enabled communication and amalgamation between the olds tribes. Moreover, some Mongol kings and Khans embraced Islam and it exerted a great influence on the spread of Islam in this region. The Hui Huis grew much stronger when the Uighurs, some of the Mongols and other tribes joined in by embracing Islam.

The national migration taking place in the Yuan Dynasty made a large number of the Hui Huis begin to live a new life dependent on farming. The preferential treatment given by the Yuan government together with their own efforts enabled Muslims to live in one place for a long period of time and maintain their life without any economic aid from the outside world. The class system practiced during the Yuan Dynasty created favorable conditions for the development of the Hui Huis. They enjoyed certain privileges on many aspects such as working in the government, paying lower taxes and attending the imperial examinations. It made it possible for different tribes and groups of the same class with the same religious belief and custom to amalgamate and become one ethic community.

It was an indication of the acknowledgment and encouragement given to Islam by the authority of the Yuan Dynasty that a good number of mosques were built as sites for Muslims' religious activities. The Mosques became a place where Muslims of various identities could come together to perform religious services and engage in various social activities. Hence, Islam became an important medium to foster and strengthen

◎ Huhehaote Mosque in Inner Mongolia.

national ties, eventually leading to the birth of the Hui Huis as an ethic group.

In the Yuan Dynasty, the distribution of the Hui Huis appeared to be "being dispersed widely and concentrated in small groups". By "being dispersed widely" the Hui Huis were scattered all over the country; and by "being concentrated in small groups"

the Hui Huis throughout the country lived in compact communities with mosques at the center of their community. The unique characteristics of the geographical distribution of the Hui Huis, different from that of other minority groups had much to do with the specific environment in which the Hui Huis lived during the Yuan Dynasty.

The Hui Huis were adept at engaging in business and managing finance and were capable of and experienced in administration. Additionally for the great contribution they had made to establish the Yuan Dynasty and administer the country, the Hui Huis won the trust of the Yuan rulers. They were given higher political status, and many of them were appointed officials at various levels. In almost all positions there were Hui Huis - civil and military, central and local, provincial and grass-root. They were in possession of land, houses, servants, subordinates and large property.

To meet the needs of the wars, the Yuan government carried

out the system of Tun Tian (having garrison troops or peasants open up wasteland and grow food grains) in its early period. When the whole country was reunified, it began to implement this system comprehensively. Among the Hui Huis who opened more wasteland and grew more grains, most were in the Northwest.

The Mongols conquered the world with their sharp cavalry, so they attached great importance to grazing horses, and opened 14 grazing lands throughout the country. Among the herdsmen who were engaged in military horse grazing, many were Hui Huis. Huihuiwa near to Gongxian County in Henan Province, and Yidu and Qingzhou in Shandong Province were important places where Hui Huis grazed horses. These military herdsmen were transformed into civil households afterwards and became local inhabitants.

The Yuan Dynasty also practiced the system of Jun Hu (militarized households). The government allocated lands for Jun Hus for military maintenance, and were exempt from tax. So Jun Hus were both militarized households and peasant households at the same time, who fought as soldiers did in times of war and farmed and grazed like peasants in times of peace. Most of the Hui Huis recruited into the army as gunners or craftsmen usually did not take their families, and became permanent local inhabitants when they settled down where they fought or stationed. They lived there, farming and intermarrying with local people.

The Yuan government also encouraged the Hui Huis who came along with the Mongols from the west to settle down in China to be engaged in agriculture and animal husbandry, and gave them many preferential policies such as allocating wasteland for them to cultivate, permitting them to engage in land business with favorable taxation treatment. Thus, the Hui Huis coming from the west soon became laborers who cultivated wasteland and developed agricultural production. In the Northwest in particular including Shaanxi, Gansu, Ningxia, Qinghai and Xinjiang, they lived and intermarried with local people, and eventually became permanent inhabitants there.

Among the Hui Huis coming along with the Mongols from the west there were a great number of craftsmen. For example, when the capital of Khorezm (a part of the ancient Persian Empire, conquered by the Arabs around 700 A.D., and by the Mongols in the 13th century, now in Uzbekistan) was destroyed, over 100 thousand craftsmen were sent to China, and more than 30 thousand craftsmen captured in the Battle of Samarkand were moved to China and settled down in compact areas too.

During the Yuan period, Hui Hui traders who came along with the Mongols from the west and Muslim traders from Southeast Asia were everywhere in the country. Traffic became convenient after the Mongols' conquering marches to the west, and motivated by the preferential treatment, Hui Hui traders came to China in large numbers and in the end settled down where they worked.

The Yuan Dynasty was appreciative of the scientific talents of the Hui Huis who came from the west and put them in important positions. To make good use of these professionals, the Yuan government set up special departments to deal with certain work, for example Guang Hui Si (department of wide welfare) was in charge of the Hui Huis' medicine; Hui Hui Guo Zi Jian (the Imperial College of the Hui Huis) was for training translators; and Hui Hui Si Tian Jian (astronomy department of the Hui Huis) was in charge of the management and study of the Hui Huis' astronomy and calendar system. Many Hui Hui experts like astronomer Jamal al-Din and Kamal al-Din, artillery-making expert 'Ala' al-Din and Isma'il, architect Ihteer al-Din, medical scientist Dalima, and linguist Haluddin were placed in various institutions established by the imperial court.

The Yuan rulers held an attitude of tolerance and protection towards all religions. Islam developed rapidly at that time. The Mongols' conquering marches to the west and the religious policies they adopted directly promoted the extensive spread and development of Islam in the Northwest of China and Central Asia, and made Islam develop into the religion that was later to be in a leading position.

· · · · · · · · · · · · · · ·

3. Religious System of Islam in China and the Development of Mosques

As more Hui Huis continued coming in from the west, Islam spread widely to the Chinese interior. The system of Fan Fang (foreign settlement) practiced in the Tang and Song periods became less efficient in administrating religious and ethnic affairs in the Yuan Dynasty. So the Department of Qadi was set up in both central and local governments to be in charge specifically of the interior matters of the Hui Huis and their religious affairs. Wherever the Hui Huis were of large number, a local Department of Qadi was set up to handle religious, civil and penal affairs among Muslims.

Qadi is a word originated from Arabic, meaning executive officer of Islamic Law, who is authorized to judge civil, commercial and penal affairs among Muslims in accordance with Islamic law. During the first half of the Yuan period, Qadi was the supreme religious personnel of Islam, who was preacher, religious leader, judicial and executive officer and commander of Muslims as well. He enjoyed very high religious and social status, and was respectfully called master by the court.

The Department of Qadi that appeared in the Yuan Dynasty was composed of a certain number of Qadis, whose responsibility was to pray for good fortune for the emperor, deal with religious affair, preach at gathering prayers, judge on religious, civil and penal affairs among the Muslims in accordance with Islamic law, and administrate Islamic internal matters.

Qadis were both government officials and Muslims' religious leaders. Therefore, the system of Qadi was a combination of religion with politics and autonomy to some extent. To set up the Department of Qadi for the first time in the Yuan Dynasty, the emperor issued an imperial order to ratify it and specify its functions and powers so as to govern all Muslims in China.

During the mid and late period of the Yuan Dynasty (mid-14th century), the Department of Qadi was eventually abolished, but Qadis still existed. They were not in charge of praying for good fortune for the country and the emperors any longer, but still functioned as judges to settle judicial matters among Muslims until the end of the Yuan Dynasty.

The establishment of the Department of Qadi was of great

◎ Exterior of Zhenjiang Mosque.

importance to the further development of Islam in China. What Qadis did in the Yuan Dynasty such as praying for good fortune for the Non-Muslim Mongol emperors and eulogizing their wisdom and bravery, laid the theoretic foundation for the Theory of Double Loyalties (loyal to Allah, and loyal to the supreme ruler as well), a theory advanced by the Hui scholars in Ming and Qing period.

As the Muslim population and the number of the mosques kept increasing, it became increasingly necessary to satisfy the needs of Muslims' religious life. Thereupon, the system of Qadi changed, and a new system called "Triple-Party Administration" came into being.

"Triple-Party Administration" means three parties, namely Imam, Khatib and Mu'adhdhin together administrate Islamic affairs. This system was established in the Ming Dynasty. It was a creation of Chinese Islam and rare in Islamic countries and regions. It was also the result of the development and evolution of Islam in Chinese historical conditions.

As the Department of Qadi was eventually abolished during the mid to late period of the Yuan Dynasty, Jiao Fang (Muslim settlement) took its place. Jiao Fang was actually a special type

© Interior of Zhenjiang Mosque.

of organization without any official nature. It was neither an executive institution on certain levels nor subordinate to any executive institutions, but a sort of religious organization for Muslims' common religious activities within the imperial system. It was characterized by:1) Jiao Fangs were independent to each other, not subordinate to each other; 2) they were exclusive, not related to each other; 3) each Jiao Fang took a mosque as center and organized a community that covered religious, political, economic, cultural and civil affairs and social activities; 4) the affairs of Jiao Fang were separated from that of the mosque but related to it to some extent.

This sort of organization appeared in cities first. As the policy of combining the army with peasants was put into practice in the Yuan Dynasty, Jiao Fangs also appeared in the countryside. The mosque was the core of Jiao Fang, and the basic condition for its birth and growth.

In the Yuan Dynasty, mosques were built wherever the Muslims were concentrated throughout the country. It was a symbol that Islam had successfully taken root in China. As a religious site, mosque played an important role in intensifying Muslims' faith and educating Muslims to perform religious services and fulfill religious assignments. It was in control of the Muslims' spiritual world in a sense. In the Yuan Dynasty the site where Muslims performed prayers (actually mosques) did not yet have a fixed name. They were called by different names such as "Li Bai Si" (prayer temple), "Hui Hui Si" (Hui Huis' temple), "Hui Hui Tang" (Hui Huis' hall), "Zhen Jiao Si" (temple of revealed religion) or "Qing Jing Si" (clear and clean temple). Compared to that in Tang and Song period, the function of the

mosque became more diversified during the Yuan Dynasty. It was not only a place where the Muslims performed prayers, but also a rostrum where they learned and preached Islam, also a public place where the Imam and other Islamic leaders handled the internal matters of the

© Zhenjiao Mosque in Qingzhou, Shangdong.

community, a place where Muslims commemorated the old sages of the past, and also a service center where Muslims could seek help on many things. Later it developed into the center of Mosque Education (Islamic education conducted in mosques). As the system of Jiao Fang developed and matured, the economic and public welfare and free schools within Jiao Fang developed and emerged one after another, making the mosque which was the center of Jiao Fang an important place for the Muslims' social life. Innumerable mosques were built or rebuilt during the Yuan and early Ming dynasties (the 13th century to the middle of the 14th century). Unfortunately, due to wars and natural disasters, many of them have been destroyed. The ones still in existence today are of the following: the Zheng Jiao (or Feng Huang) Mosque in Hangzhou, the Song Jiang Mosque in Shanghai, the Nan Cheng Mosque and the Yong Nian Mosque in Kunming, the Qing Zhen Mosque in Fuzhou, the Zhen Jiao Mosque in Qingzhou, Shandong, the Hua Jue Mosque in Xi'an, the Jing Jue Mosque in Nanjing, the Great Southern Mosque in Jinan, the Niu Jie Mosque and the Dong Si Mosque in Beijing.

4. *Concentration and Dispersion of Islam in the Chinese Inland*

During the first two hundred years of the Ming Dynasty (around the late 14th century to the early 16th century), the coverage of Islam further expanded in China. New compact communities with mosques as center emerged one after another. The Muslims in the inland moved to medium and small cities, towns and countryside in various ways, and led to the birth of comparatively stable compact communities of Muslims in places, even in some remote areas, where there were no such communities before, such as Jining, Linqing, Dezhou, Botou and Cangzhou which are located on the northern bank of the Canal from Beijing to Hangzhou, Changping, Tianjin, Qian'an, Yixian, and Baoding around Beijing, and Lingzhou, Tongxin and Guyuan in Ningxia. Also in this case were Guizhou Province and Tibet. And Weishan, Baoshan, Tengchong, Songming, Zhanyi, Qujing, Yuxi, Mengzi and Shiping in Yunnan Province were also places where Muslims moved in only since the early Ming Dynasty.

In the Ming Dynasty (1368-1644 A.D.), the Muslim population grew fastest in Nanjing, capital of the Ming Dynasty. Nanjing was called Jiankang Lu in the Yuan Dynasty (1206-1368 A.D.), having jurisdiction over Lushi Si (now southern part of Nanjing) and five counties Jiangning, Shangyuan, Jurong, Lishui and Liyang. By the 27th year of the Yuan Dynasty (1290 A.D.), there were 163 households of Se Mu (one of the four classes into which China's population was divided in the Yuan Dynasty) in Lushi Si, Jiangning and Shangyuan. The Hui Huis were only a part of Se Mu people at that time, whose population did not even reach one thousand atlthough it accounted for one third of the Se Mu population.

In the early Ming period however, the population of the Hui Huis increased greatly. By the 2nd year of Wanli (1592 A.D.), the total number of households in Jiangning, a county of Nanjing, was 3239, among which 9230 persons were Hui Huis. By the period of Hongwu, the Hui Hui population in Jiangning grew to 100,000, ten times as many as that in the period of Wanli. If other counties of Nanjing were taken into account, the total population of the Hui Huis in Nanjing was quite large. The main reason why the Hui Hui population increased at such a sharp speed in Nanjing was that a large number of the Hui Huis moved

◎ Tongxin Mosque in Ningxia (said to be built in the Ming Dynasty).

in from other places in various ways.

Firstly, many Hui Hui generals and soldiers who had joined the Ming army and those of the Yuan army who surrendered to the Ming moved to Nanjing. In the last years of the Yuan Dynasty, many Hui Huis participated in the wars to overthrow the Yuan Dynasty, and some of them were promoted to very high positions for their merit. When the Ming Dynasty was founded, many Hui Huis such as Chang Yuchun, Mu Ying, Lan Yu, Feng Sheng, Hu Dahai, Tang He, Deng Yu, were ranked among princes and marquises. The surrendered Muslim generals of the Yuan army also settled down in Nanjing, about which we can find evidence in the stele inscription titled "Building the Jing Jue Mosque and the Li Bai Mosque by Imperial Order in the South of Ying Tian (Nanjing was called Ying Tian in the Ming Dynasty)" written by Wang Ao in the 5th year of Hong Zhi, which says that Zhu Yuanzhang (Ming's first emperor) had the Jing Jue Mosque built in the 21st year of Hong Wu (reign title of Emperor Zhu Yuanzhang) to arrange the surrendered Muslim generals and facilitate their religious life. However, they were permitted to practise Islam and perform prayers only, not to participate in politics.

The Jing Jue Mosque is the only ancient mosque still in existence in Nanjing today. As it was located in the San Shan Jie Street, it was called the San Shan Jie Mosque at first. In accordance with historic documents the Jing Jue Mosque was built in the Ming Dynasty, and covered an area of 67 hectares with its southern edge at Lin Guan Jie, western edge at Ma Xiang, eastern edge at San Shan Jie and northern edge at Sha Zhu Xiang. In later years, it was repeatedly damaged and reduced in area after renovations. According to legend the name of the Jing Jue Mosque is connected to Zhu Yuanzhang, founder of the Ming Dynasty (on the throne 1368-1398 A.D.). Legend has it that among the Hui Huis in Nanjing: Chang Yuchun, Hu Dahai and other Muslims generals often went to the San Shan Jie Mosque for prayer. One day, Zhu Yuanzhang went to the Mosque to look for them for an important matter. Seeing them performing prayer in the hall, he stepped in without thinking. According to Islamic Law, no one could enter prayer hall with shoes, so the mosque server standing aside asked him to take off his shoes, and Zhu Yuanzhang took his foot back. After that, the Mosque was renamed Jing Jue when he ordered to rebuilt it. ('Jing Jue' literally means clean and conscious, its pronunciation is similar to 'Jin Jiao' (pronounced as Jin Jue in the Nanjing dialect) which means to step foot inside)

Secondly, Hui Hui craftsmen, traders, warriors and various professionals moved to Nanjing.

◎ Exquisite brick carving of Jingjue Mosque in Nanjing.

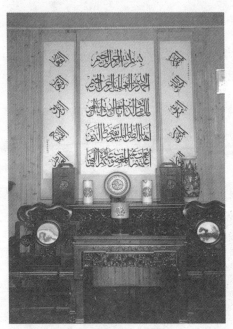

◎ Old furniture and Arabic calligraphy in Jingjue Mosque in Nanjing.

During the early period of the Ming Dynasty, Nanjing was the political, economic, commercial and cultural center of the country. A large number of Hui Hui craftsmen and traders moved here. It is written in the preface of the family tree of Mr. Liang, a bone doctor living in Nanjing now, that his earliest ancestor, an expert at resetting broken bones, moved from Hulongdi in the Western Region to Biandu in the period of Xi Ning (1068-1077 A.D.) of the Song Dynasty, and the emperor of Song bestowed upon him the family name of 'Liang'. In the period of Hong Wu (1368-1398 A.D.) of the Ming Dynasty, his descendents moved to Nanjing from Biandu. There were a tremendous number of professionals among the Hui Huis in the Yuan Dynasty, and the Liangs were just one of them. Besides craftsmen, many of those coming to Nanjing were traders, especially jewelers. As the capital city where the nobility lived and the site of the country's biggest jewelry market, Nanjing attracted a lot of Hui Hui jewelers. Even in modern times Nanjing's jewelry market was still monopolized by the Hui Huis. According to the records of the family trees of the Zhengs, Wus and Mas in Nanjing, their ancestors Zheng He, Wu Ru and Ma Shayihei all moved to Nanjing from other places in the early period of the Ming Dynasty. Of course, among the Hui Huis who moved to Nanjing in this period only few could leave their names in historic records, while many more lack records today.

Zheng He (1371-1435 A.D.), whose original name was Ma Sanbao, was a famous Muslim sailor and diplomat in the Ming Dynasty. He was born to an eminent aristocratic family that had been Muslims for generations. His grandfather Char Midina was made Marquis of Dianyang in the Yuan Dynasty, and his father Milijin succeeded him as Marquis of Dianyang later. As his father and grandfather had performed Hajj to Mecca, they were respectfully called Hajji Ma. In the 14th year of Hong Wu, when Ming troops commanded by Lan Yu and Mu Ying attacked Yunnan, then under the rule of Yuan aristocrats, Zheng He was captured and sent to Nanjing. Emperor Zhu Yuanzhang gave him to Zhu Di, prince of Yan, as a eunuch. In the Battle of Jingnan, a

为纪念穆斯林航海家郑和下西洋五八〇年，
中国政府特发行纪念邮票一套

Chinese Government issued a special set of stemps to
commemorate the 580 anniversary of Muslim sailor
Zheng He's sailing to South Pacific and Indian Oceans

◎ A set of stamps commemorating Muslim sailor Zheng He.

battle between Zhu Di and Zhu Yun for the throne, Zheng He
rendered extraordinary service with his wisdom and tactics. Zhu
Di appreciated this very much and decreed an important position
upon him. In the 2nd year of Yong Le (1404 A.D.), Zhu Di, who
had taken over the throne, bestowed him Zheng as his family
name and called him Zheng He. Later, he was promoted to be
the garrison command of Nanjing.

To show the power and influence of the Ming Dynasty and
attract foreign tributes, emperor Zhu Di (1402-1424 A.D. on the
throne) decided to dispatch a large fleet on a diplomatic mission
to the countries in the Pacific and Indian Oceans. In the 3rd year
of Yong Le (1405 A.D., Yong Le is the reign title of Emperor
Zhu Di), the first sailing was launched with Zheng He as

ambassador and Wang Jinghong as vice ambassador. By the 8th year of Xuan De (1433 A.D.), within a period of 28 years, Zheng He had made seven sailings to the Pacific and Indian Oceans, leading then the largest fleet in the world, with 27,000 people aboard, including soldiers, sailors, workmen, translators and doctors. According to "History of Ming", the largest ship of his fleet was 44.4 zhangs (about 148 meters) long, 18 zhangs (about 60 meters) wide, with 9 masts and 12 sails. The ships were fully loaded with precious goods and famous products from China such as gold, silver, silk, porcelain, iron wares, cloth, tea, jade carvings and bronze coins of the Ming. They traded with local people wherever they went. Covering a total distance of over 70,000 kilometers, Zheng He visited more than 30 countries in Southeast Asia, Indian Ocean, Persian Gulf, Red Sea and the east coast of Africa. Among the countries and places he visited, Islamic countries included: Java, Malaysia, Brunei, Philippines, India, Iran, Yemen, Oman, Somalia, Kenya, Saudi Arabia, Bangladesh, Egypt. Translators aboard such as Ma Huan, Guo Chongli, Fei Xin, Ha San and Sha Ban were Muslim. In the 8th year of Xuan De (1433 A.D.), when Zheng He made his seventh sailing as far as Jeddah on the east shore of the Red Sea, he sent 7 people including the translators who believed in Islam, to Mecca for pilgrimage, and had them draw a picture of Ka'bah and took it to Nanjing. Zheng He also drew up navigation maps of his voyages, marking in detail the courses they sailed through, the geographical situations of the coasts and the ports of the countries they sailed by, and the submerged reefs, shallows, islands, mountains and coastal terrains. It is the first world map of marine geography in China. Ma Huan, Fei Xin and Gong Zhen who sailed with Zheng He detailed what they had seen and heard during their voyages in the books "Ying Ya Sheng Lan" (beautiful scenery in the far oceans), "Xing Cha Sheng Lan" (beautiful scenery seen in sailing) and "Xi Yang Fan Guo Zhi" (countries in the Pacific and Indian Occeans) respectively. They recorded the mountains, rivers, climates, products, social structures, politics, religions and traditions of various countries and places in Asia and Africa they had been to. These books are of very important documentary value to us today.

Zheng He's seven sailings opened a sea-route to east Africa across the Indian Ocean, promoted economic and cultural exchanges between China and foreign countries, and enhanced the friendly contacts between the people of China and Asian and African countries. After Zheng He's diplomatic sailings, more than 30 Asian and African countries dispatched envoys to visit

China, among whom there were 10 kings. For example, in 1417 A.D. King of Sulu (now Philippines), who was a Muslim, came to visit China and died in China afterwards and was buried in Dezhou, Shandong Province. In Southeast Asia there still exist some relics left by Zheng He. The tomb containing his personal effects is located at the south foot of Niushou Mount in Jiangning district, Nanjing. People call it Ma Hui Hui Mu (tomb of Hui Hui Ma) because Zheng He's original family name was Ma, and his father whose name was Ma Hama was called Hajj Ma. The mount where his tomb is located is called Hui Hui Mount.

To sum it up, the Hui Huis experienced a process of large-scale gathering to Nanjing in the early Ming Dynasty, but it was very short and followed by a big dispersion soon after. Some of the Hui Huis went along with the conquering army to the west, some moved to Beijing along with Emperor Yong Le, and others still moved as the capital city was moved from Nanjing to Beijing. Some of the Hui Huis living in Gansu, Qinghai, Guangxi, Yunnan and Hunan now say that their ancestors originally lived in Nanjing, and moved to these places for the above reasons during the Ming Dynasty.

The big gathering to Nanjing and big dispersion that the Hui Huis experienced in the early Ming Dynasty is of great importance for the wide spread of Islam, especially to places where Islam had never touched during the Yuan Dynasty. The Muslims population in Nanjing increased as a result, and became the city where Muslims lived most intensively on the southeast coast of China.

CHAPTER 2
NATIONALIZATION OF ISLAM IN CHINA

1. Ten Minority Groups and Two Systems

The coverage of Islam expanded widely in China as it had spread
and developed in the Tang (618-907 A.D.), Song (960-1279 A.D.),
Yuan (1206-1368 A.D.) and early Ming (1368-1644 A.D.)
dynasties. After the middle of the Ming Dynasty, fundamental
changes took place to the conditions for Islam to spread and
develop in China. First of all, the Hui Huis' political status
changed, reduced to that of being ruled from that of being second
highest class in the Yuan Dynasty. Secondly, the Ming rulers
pursued a policy of favoring agriculture and restricting trade, so
the Hui Huis lost their advantage on trading, and it led to the

decline of their economic and social status. Thirdly, the distribution structure of the Hui Huis' population characterized by "big dispersion and small concentration" obstructed the contacts among the communities in different places. Furthermore, the Ming Dynasty pursued broad national assimilation and put restriction on marriage within the same race. It forced the Hui Huis to use the Chinese language, and their national language lost its value of practice gradually. Fourthly, Jiao Fangs (Muslim settlement) that appeared as Islam developed in China began to play an important role at that time. They gathered the dispersed Hui Huis into groups with similar features, and by Islamic belief and traditions made them a new national community which had common values, ethics and customs.

Affected by the above factors, the Hui Hui community in China evolved into ten ethic groups and two systems: the Uighurs, the Kazaks, the Khalkhas, the Uzbeks, the Tajiks and the Tatars living mainly in The Xinjiang Uighur Autonomous Region, and the Huis, the Salas, the Dongxiangs and the Bao'ans living mainly in the Chinese inland.

◎ Yili Mosque in Xinjiang.

1. THE UIGHURS

"Uighur" literally means "unite" or "ally". The ethnic origin of the Uighurs can be traced back to the 3rd century B.C. Their ancestors believed in Shamanism, Manicheism, Nestorianism, Mazdaism and Buddhism. The Uighurs are distributed mainly in The Xinjiang Uighur Autonomous Region, while a small portion live in Hunan and Henan Provinces. The present population of the Uighurs is about 7.2 million. In the middle of the 10th century, Islam was introduced to Xinjiang as Satuk Boghra (910-956 A.D.), khan of the Karakitai Dynasty embraced Islam. Kashgar, Yirqiang and Kuche became Islamic one after another after. After the 14th century Islam spread to the north of Xinjiang, and by the 16th century, the whole region became Islamic. The Eidkah Mosque in Kashgar, the Mazar of Afaq Khwadja, the tomb of the Uighur King in Hami and the Emin Minaret in Turufan all are Islamic constructions dating from early times. The Uighur Muslims are hospitable and adept at singing and dancing. Their beautiful folk art works, including the epic poem "Fu Le Zhi Hui" (wisdom and happiness) and the music and dance divertimento "Shi Er Mu Ka Mu" (twelve Mukams) are still popular at present. The Uighurs are engaged mainly in agriculture, being experienced in gardening and cotton growing.

◎ Colorful furniture and decoration of the Uighurs' house.

They are also adept at carpet weaving, Uighur cap and knife making.

2. THE KAZAKS

The Kazaks are distributed mainly over Yili, Tacheng and A'ertai in the Xinjiang Uighur Autonomous Region with a population of 1.2 million. It is an amalgamation of several ancient minority groups living in the north of China. By the middle of

the 15th century when the Kazak Khanate was founded, the Kazaks came into being as an ethic group. Islam was introduced to the Kazak Grassland rather early, and spread widely after the 18th century. The Islamic doctrine was written in "Tou Ke Corpus Juris", the

◎ Kazak women and children living in the Tianshan Mountains.

national corpus juris of the Kazaks. There appeared in the history a number of Kazak mullahs and scholars who were well versed in both Islam and Arabic. The Kazaks are affluent in folklore, with the outstanding epics "Alpamis", "Kobuland" and "Salih and Saman". They like music, and are adept at singing and dancing. Donbura is their representative musical instrument. The

Kazaks are engaged mainly in animal husbandry and a little agriculture as well, and some of them are engaged in industry and commerce.

3. THE KHALKHAS

The Khalkhas is also an ancient ethnic group living in the Xinjiang Uighur Autonomous Region, who allied with the Uighurs, the Kazaks and the Mongols and cooperated with the army of the Qing Dynasty to put down the rebellions of the Elder

◎ Khalkhas Muslims who are adept at both singing and dancing.

and Younger Khwajas, and maintained the union of China. They live mainly in the Ke'erlesu Khalkhas Autonomous Prefecture in Xinjiang with a population of 140,000. They are engaged mainly in animal husbandry and a little agriculture as well. They have very beautiful folklore, legends and vivid sayings with unique national characteristics. The famous epic poem "Manas" is a treasure of their folk art. The Khalkhas women are adept at handicraft such as embroidery, carpet and mural production.

4. THE UZBEKS

The Uzbeks are scattered in places such as Urumchi, Kashgar, Yining and Tacheng in the Xinjiang Uighur Autonomous Region, with a population of about 15,000. Around the 15th century, they settled down in China and embraced Islam. They use phonetic letters based on Arabic, which makes it much easier for them to study Islam. The Uzbeks have built some large

◎ An Uzbek family living in the basin of the Yili River.

mosques in Kashgar, Shache, Yili and Qitai. Most of the Uzbeks are engaged in commerce. The Uzbeks in southern Xinjiang are very skillful at silk weaving while the ones in northern Xinjiang are adept at animal husbandry.

5. THE TAJIKS

The Tajiks have a population of about 33,000, being of European origin. They are concentrated in the Tashkurkan Tajik Autonomous County, east of Pamir, and a small number live in Shache, Zepu, Yecheng and Aketao. In the 11th century, their ancestors were converted into sect Ismail of Shiah, and they still abide by the law of this sect now. The Tajiks are engaged mainly in animal husbandry and farming. They have literature with a long historic tradition. "Shah Nameh" (book of kings) by the famous Persian classic poet Firdawsi still

© A Tajik youth playing a pleasant melody for new life.

spreads among them. As the Tajiks live on plateaus, their literature works always concern hawks.

6. THE TATARS

The Tatars are the descendents of several Turki nomadic tribes subjected to the Turki Khanate Empire during the Tang Dynasty. Around the 1820's and 1830's, they moved to Xinjiang

◎ A family get-together of the Tatars.

from the Sino-Russia border. Most of the Tatars are businessmen, while some are engaged in Islamic education in places such as Yining and Tacheng. The population of the Tatars is 5-6,000. Those of the Tatars living in city mainly engage in business, medical care and education, while the ones in the countryside are engaged in farming, especially beekeeping. The Tatars are comparatively well educated with the highest percentage of intellectualization among all the nationalities in China. The Tatar School in Yining is the earliest new type ethic school. The literature works of the Tatars are characterized by that of the Uighurs, Russians and Uzbeks. They are adept at singing and dancing, having many types of musical instruments.

7. THE HUIS

The ancestors of the Huis are the Arab and Persian Muslim envoys, traders and travelers who came and settled down in China in the period of the Tang and Song dynasties, who first brought Islam to China. As early as the beginning of the 13th century, many people in Central Asia came to China along with the Mongol army. They scattered all over the country as garrison troops, craftsmen, traders or scholars, being called Hui Hui then. The Huis began to use Chinese from the Ming Dynasty, but Imams still spoke Arabic when presiding over religious services and this tradition has been in practice up till now. The Huis are not considerably distinguished from the Hans in dress. The Huis in the countryside live mainly on farming and take commerce

◎ A wedding ceremony of the Huis.

and handicraft industries as sideline industries, while the ones living in towns and cities are mainly engaged in small businesses such as catering trade, coat processing.

The Huis have a population of 8.6 million, being one of the minority groups with largest population and coverage. They are scattered almost in every province, city and autonomous region, while many more are concentrated in the Ningxia Hui Autonomous Region, Qinghai Province, Gansu Province, Shaanxi Province, the Xinjiang Uighur Autonomous Region, Yunnan Province, Hebei Province, Henan Province, Shandong Province and Inner Mongolia Autonomous Region. There is one autonomous region, namely the Ningxia Hui Autonomous Region, two autonomous prefectures and eleven autonomous counties for the Huis in the whole country.

8. THE SALAS

The Salas live in the Xunhua Sala Autonomous County, Qinghai Province, with a population of 900,000. They have their own national spoken language, but no written language. Their ancestors were a branch of the Saruks who lived in the 13th century, belonging to the west Turki Oguz tribe in Samarkand. A chieftain named Kharmang led the clan men believing in Islam eastwards to Xunhua, Qinghai, and settled down there and lived and intermarried with the local Tibetans and Hans and multiplied, and becoming an ethnic group. The Salas are mainly engaged in farming and take animal husbandry and gardening as sideline industries. They have preserved much beautiful folklore. Duiwina (camel game), a traditional game showing how their ancestors came to Xunhua from Central Asia, is very popular among the Salas.

9. THE DONGXIANGS

The Dongxiangs live in the Dongxiang Autonomous County

◎ Dongxiang Muslims frying pies.

in Linxia prefecture of Gansu Province with a population of 370 thousand. The main body of their ethnic origin is Se Mu (one of the four classes into which China's population was divided in the Yuan Dynasty, including Central Asian allies of the Mongols, mostly Uighurs and other Turks.) who came with the Mongol army to China in the 13th century and settled down in Dongxiang. They are also related to the Huis, the Mongols and the Hans in blood. There are comparatively more sects and Menhuans (Sufist sects in China) among the Dongxiangs, each having its own mosque. The doctrine and tradition of each sect and Menhuan is fully implemented in the daily life of the Dongxiangs. They still preserve very well the transcript of the Holy Qur'an brought from the Central Asia by their ancestors. The Dongxiangs are engaged mainly in farming. They are affluent in folklore, with epics "Miraqah and Girl Mazhilu" and "Pu Tao E Er" (grape moth). Like the Huis, the Dongxiangs are fond of singing Hua'er (a kind of folk song, popular in Gansu, Qinghai and Ningxia).

10. THE BAO'ANS

The Bao'ans are also called Bao'an Huis. They have their own national spoken language, but no written language. They

© Exquisite and useful belt knives produced by Bao'an Muslims.

are concentrated in Jishishan County in Linxia Prefecture with a population of 15,000. Their ancestors were the Mongols and the Hui Huis in Central Asia who came to China around the later period of the Yuan Dynasty and early Ming Dynasty. They were sent to garrison the frontier in Tongue, Qinghai at first, and settled down there and intermarried with the local Tibetans and Hans, and eventually became an ethnic group. There are mosques in every village where the Bao'ans live. They have similar customs to the Huis, Dongxiangs and Salas. The Bao'ans live on farming, and Bao'an Knife making is their traditional handicraft industry. They are dressed similarly with the Huis living in the Northwest.

All the above ten minority groups who take Islam as their national religious belief are members of the Chinese nation without exception. By combining Islam with their national traditions and culture, they have made the Chinese Islamic culture more diversified. This new phenomenon of religious culture has raised intense interest among social scientists both home and abroad.

To adapt themselves to Chinese culture, the Muslims in China evolved into ten ethnic groups with different characteristics.

◎ Exquisite handicrafts made by Chinese Muslims.

The Muslims of the Huis, Salas, Dongxiangs and Bao'ans were the descendants of the traders who came to China by the Silk Roads both over land and sea, and the soldiers and craftsmen who came inland with the Mongol army or the Muslims who migrated from the Western Region. They either lived in China engaging in business or were arranged in compact areas, intermarrying with other ethnic groups and multiplying. Islam, as a life style and faith, was spread to various places in a peacefully way along with the Muslims' movement from one place to another. Islam played a very important role in the births of the above nationalities and was the core factor in their development. Among the Huis, Salas, Dongxiangs and Bao'ans, the Huis have the largest population and coverage, and highest mobility. After the Ming Dynasty (1368-1644 A.D.), six major regions where the Huis lived in compact communities came into being, namely the south of the Yangtze River with Nanjing and Suzhou as center, Gan Ning Qing (Gansu, Ningxia and Qinghai) area with Hezhou, Didao and Xining as center, Guanzhong (Shaanxi) area with Chang'an as center, Yunnan area, Ji Lu Yu (Hebei, Shandong and Henan) area with Beijing as center and other area.

The Uighurs, Kazaks, Khalkhas, Uzbeks, Tajiks and Tatars live mainly in the Xinjiang Uighur Autonomous Region. This is a place with a large area, many ethic groups and many religions. Xinjiang is related to neighboring Islamic countries in many aspects such as ethnic origin, religion, economy, culture and customs, but has never broken away from the central authority in any way. It was by various means such as the Da'wah, religious war against Buddhism and political support here, that Islam spread. Compared to the places where Huis and other nationalities live, the conditions, method and manifestation for the spread and development of Islam are completely different here.

First of all, the rise and decline of Khwaja (a large family in

Xinjiang then)-Ishan (a sect of Islam in Xinjiang then) power exerted direct influence on the regime of Xinjiang practicing a system of combining religion with politics. Around the 13th century, the descendents of Shuzauddin, a mullah in Bukhara exiled to Karakorum by Jenghis Khan, and the ancestor of Mullah Khwaja Osiddin came to Luobu Quetai (located between Turufan and Yutian) to spread the doctrine of Ishan. In later years, Khwaja-Ishan power continued to grow, and gradually developed from a religious power into a secular regime, which existed until Xinjiang was reunified by the Qing Dynasty. Compared to that of the Chinese inland, this was a completely different precondition for Islam's existence and development.

Secondly, Khwaja-Ishan worship prevailed. The Khwaja family enjoyed the status of Ishan, while Ishan bore the identity of Khwaja. Due to the vigorous support of the Khwaja family, Ishan obtained full development in Xinjiang and received much more secular power and allowed Islam to penetrate into all aspects of the Uighurs' social life as a result. In the 15th-17th century, Ishan became the main pillar of the serf system practiced in the Uighur region. As the main content of Khwaja-Ishan worship, building and worshiping Mazar (mausoleum) prevailed here. Xinjiang is well known in the Islamic world for its Mazars with a wide coverage, large number and amazing diversity, and also for the mystical legends of the buried and the complicated content of Mazar worship. Khwaja-Ishan combined saint worship with Mazar worship, making Mazar a shrine and an important religious site. However, the real reason why they did this was simply to induce believers to pay stronger worship to the living Khwaja-Ishan and achieve their actual economic and political interests. It was in these circumstances that Khwaja-Ishan power was secularized and feudalized.

Thirdly, religious education achieved unprecedented development. Early in the 10th century, the first Islamic institution of higher learning in Chinese Islamic history was set up in Kashgar. In subsequent dynasties, 10 Islamic institutes were built and some older historic institutes were renovated. These institutes were of considerable scale, offering courses such as Arabic, Persian, Qur'anic annotation, dogmatics, Islamic Law, Islamic history, logic, Arabic grammar, poems of Sufism and works of Islamic philosophers. A large number of religious professionals and literary talents were produced in these institutes and the influence of Islam continued to expand as a result.

During this period of time, the King of Hami and his family practiced temporal-religious administration over the Uighur

© A busy Muslim bazaar in Xinjiang.

Muslims within his territory, similar to that of khans and Khwaja-Ishan regime.

After Tuhiru Timur and his 160,000 Mongol subjects embraced Islam, all the khans after him were Muslim. They forcibly ejected other religions out of Turufan and Islam occupied the spiritual world of the Uighurs. By the early 16th century, Islam had taken the predominant position in Hami, symbolizing that the entire nation of the Uighurs in Xinjiang had by then embraced Islam. After the mid and late Ming Dynasty period, peoples such as the Kazaks to the north of Tianshan Mountain accepted Islam one after another.

The two systems of Islam in China (Islam in the inland with the Huis as representative, and Islam in Xinjiang with the Uighurs as representative) differed considerably from each other during this early period. Until the mid and late Qing Dynasty, as the policy of separating religion from politics was put into practice, the two systems tended to develop in pace with each other. As many Huis moved to Xinjiang as garrison troops or migrants, and economic contacts between the farming area in south Xinjiang and the pasturing area in north Xinjiang became closer, their economy tended to grow at the same pace. As Islam itself changed and religion became separated from politics, the function of Shariah (Islamic law) changed as well. As Khwaja-Ishan power declined, the differences between major sects vanished, and peoples such as the Uighurs became Muslims, the two systems of Islam in China tended to be identical in pattern of sects in the early 20th century.

Of course, Islam in both Xinjiang and the inland will continue to develop in ways of their own, so far as the influence of comparatively stable factors such as ethnic background and geography is concerned.

2.Birth and Growth of Sects and Menhuans

Before the transition period between the Qing and Ming dynasties (mid-17th century), Muslims in China belonged to the Sunni sect, except the Tajiks who were of the Shiah sect and a very small number of the Uighurs who believed in Ithna Ashariyyah. As for the schools they followed, except a few in Xinjiang following Shafi'iyyah, the rest were of Hanafiyyah. In the transition period between Ming and Qing dynasties, as Sufism was introduced into China, many independent sects and Menhuans emerged one after another and grew rapidly, among which three sects: Qadim, Ikhwan and Xidaotang, and four Menhuans: Kubrawiyyah, Qadiriyyah, Khufiyyah and Jahriyyah were of greatest influence.

Qadim, which means "traditional sect", is a sect of Islam in China that has spread early and widely and has more followers and greater influence than any other sect. As it adheres to the teachings, thoughts and ceremonies that have been practiced for generations since the Tang and Song dynasties, so it was named

Qadim. Qadim is of Sunni. It bases its religious thoughts upon the Holy Qur'an and strictly abides by the "Six Beliefs", "Eight Ultimate Principles" and traditional ceremonies and proprieties. It holds an attitude of respect and tolerance towards others sects and schools, and coexists in peace with other religions prevailing in China. Having undergone a long process of development in Song, Yuan, Ming and Qing dynasties, Qadim has become the mainstream sect of Islam in China, being unique in its own style. Qadim was influence by Shiah to some extent although it has always walked its own path. It takes Tariqah (austerity) practiced by Sufism as Tatawwu, does not worship saints and their mausoleums but is not firmly opposed to it on the other hand. On the aspect of its etiquette and customs, there are some things borrowed from the culture of the Hans.

Ikhwan, which literally means brotherhood, is also called Ahl al-Sunni (a sect abiding by the Holy Qur'an) and most other sects call it the New Sect. It was established by Ma Wanfu, a well-known Dongxiang Imam in Hezhou (now the Linxia Hui Prefecture in Gansu), at the end of the 19th century. In the short time of some tens of years, it has quickly developed into a new sect covering Gansu, Ningxia and Qinghai. It abides by the doctrine of Sunni and follows the teaching of the Hanafiyyah

School, maintaining that all the etiquettes and ceremonies that are not in line with the Holy Qur'an and Hadith should be abolished. It is against mausoleum and murshid (guide) worship, and advocates that preaching and Da'wah should be done in Chinese.

Xidaotang also previously called Jinxingtang. Basing its doctrine upon the works of well-known Chinese Islamic scholars such as Liu Zhi and others, it is also called Hanxuepai (school of Chinese culture). It believes that only by combining with Chinese culture could Islam be developed in China. Xidaotang was established by Ma Qixi (1857-1914 A.D.) in a small town called Jiucheng in Lintan County, Gansu Province. It abides by the doctrine of Sunni and follows the teaching of Hanafiyyah, and takes the works of Liu Zhi and others as its Da'wah source. It attaches great importance to Mawlid al-Nabiy (birthday of Prophet Muhammad and also the day when he passed away) and the anniversary of the death of Ma Qixi, founder of Xidaotang, but did not build any mausoleums for the murshids (guide) after him. It practices murshid-domination system with the murshid as both religious head and the manager of the followers' secular life. Its followers are of two categories: individual households and collective households. The individual households are scattered all over the Northwest of China, independent on economy and living, but they can seek help from Xidaotang when they are in need. The collective households are concentrated in the home of Xidaotang located in Lintan County and engaging in business on farming, forestry, animal husbandry and commerce

© Xianhe Mosque in Yangzhou.

collectively. It calls for pursuing knowledge, encouraging all school-age boys and girls within Xidaotang itself and of all other nationalities of the locale to attend school, and selects the top students within Xidaotang to receive secondary and high education, so a considerable number of its followers are well educated. Xidaotang is a religious sect and a special economic community as well.

Menhuan is a general term for all the Sufist schools and their branches prevailing in inland China. Sufism was introduced to Xinjiang from Bukhara and Samarkand in Central Asia in the 17th century, and separated into two sects: Baishan (white mountain) and Heishan (black mountain). All the Sufi schools and branches in Xinjiang are generally called Ishan. Since the 18th century, Sufi schools such as Kubrawiyyah, Qadiriyyah, Khufiyyah and Jahriyyah (called Four Menhuans by Muslims) were introduced into Gansu, Ningxia and Qinghai successively. Influenced by traditional Chinese culture, some smaller branches such as Mufti, Dawantou, Dagongbei, Huasi, Guanchuan came into being. These Sufi schools and branches that prevailed in the areas of the Huis did not have a common name at the very beginning, so some of them continued to use the name of the sect from which they originated, such as Kubrawiyyah and Qadiriyyah; some were named according to the tone of their chanting Dhikr (praise to Allah), such as Khufiyyah and Jahriyyah; some were named after the place where the mausoleum of the founder or mosque are located, such as Bijiachang and Baizhuang; some were named after the family name of the founder, such as Xianmen and Zhangmen; some were given the name for their wide coverage and grand construction of the mausoleums, such as Dagongbei (grand mausoleum) and Huasi (splendid mosque); some were named with the word on the stele bestowed by the local government, such as Mufti.

Menhuan is a type of organization combined with religious mysticism. It is built upon a specific social and economic foundation with centralized power and a considerable sphere of influence, existing among the Huis, Dongxiangs, Salas and Bao'ans. Neither Menhuans nor their branches came into being in the same period or in the same way. When Sufism was introduced into China, four major schools were produced, namely Four Menhuans as is called usually.

Khufiyyah, Arabic transliteration, originally means "hidden" or "silent". It advocates chanting Dhikr in low tone, therefore it was named as such. It was founded by Muhammad Bahauddin (1381-1388 A.D.) who lived in Central Asia, and originated from Naqshibandiyyah. Around the 16th century, Muhammad Yusuf, grandson of Ajaam, introduced it into Xinjiang, and developed it into a sect called Baishan (white mountain). During the same period of time, Ishaq, another grandson of Ajaaam, also came to Yirqiang in Xinjing to develop his influence, and the sect founded by him is called Heishan (black mountain). In the 17th century,

◎ Minaret of Dongguan Mosque in Xining, Qinghai.

Khufiyyah was introduced into Gansu, Ningxia and Qinghai from Xinjiang and Arabia. Having undergone two hundred years of spreading, developing and amalgamating with Chinese culture, it has generated many branches. Khufiyyah abides by the doctrine of Sunni and follows the teaching of the Hanafiyyah School.

Qadiriyyah, Arabic transliteration, is named after the word appearing in the name of its founder Abd al-Qadir al-Jilani. It was established in the 12th century and prevailed in Baghdad, and developed into one of the biggest Sufi societies. During the early reign of Kang Xi of the Qing Dynasty, Khwaja Abdullah who proclaimed to be the 29th generation of Prophet Muhammad introduced Qadiriyyah into Gansu, Ningxia and Qinghai, which afterwards separated into three smaller sects: Qimen, Xianmen (converted into Khufiyyah later) and Mamen (founded by Yunnan Ma). In later years, Qadiriyyah evolved into many branches that are not subordinated to each other. In addition to the three sects of Qadiriyyah founded by Abdullah, there were other sects founded by those who had studied it in Xinjiang or Arabia and spread it in their hometown Qansu and Qinghai when they returned. Qadiriyyah abides by the doctrine of Sunni and follows the teaching of the Hanafiyyah School.

Jahriyyah, Arabic transliteration, originally means "open"

or "loud" and has by extension come to mean "chanting Dhikr loudly". So Jahriyyah is also called Sect of Loud Chanting, opposite to Khufiyyah which is called Sect of Low Chanting. In the 16th century Jahriyyah was introduced into Shache and Kashgar in Xinjiang from Central Asia. In 1744 Ma Mingxin (1719-1781 A.D.) introduced it into Gansu, Ningxia and Qinghai. The followers of Jahriyyah are distributed in the Northwest, and 13 provinces such as Yunnan, Guizhou. Followers of it number among the Donggans (descendants of the Huis who immigrated to Russia and Central Asia). Jahriyyah abides by the doctrine of Sunni and follows the teaching of the Hanafiyyah School.

Kubrawiyyah, Arabic transliteration, originated from the Kubrawi Society founded by the Persian Sufi philosopher Najimddin Kubrawi in the 13th century. In accordance with historic records that the first one who introduced Kubrawiyyah into China was a foreign missionary named Muhaaiddin. He came to China three times, firstly to Guangdong and Guangxi, secondly to Hunan and Hubei and thirdly to Gansu. Finally he settled down in Dawantou, a village in Dongxiang, Hezhou, in the transition period of the Ming and Qing dynasties. He took a Chinese name and worked on a land of 0.9 hectares presented by the villagers, and became a member of the Dongxiangs in the end. Along with him came his son Ahmad Junayd Naqshiband Baghdadi, who became the second murshid (guide) of Kubrawiyyah and converted more followers including a small number of the Hans. Kubrawiyyah is also called Zhangmen or Dawantou Menhuan. It is of Sunni and belongs to the Hanafiyyah School. Although Menhuans differ from each other, they still have much in common.

1. Murshid worship. The followers call murshid "Lao Ren Jia" (a respectful form of address to an old man) and take him as sheikh who can guide them onto the path of righteousness, and even deem him as Wali (address to the Sufi master) who can create and manifest various Karamats (miracles). The followers pay greatest respect to murshid and ask for his Kou Huan (permission) on almost everything, becoming the master of both their secular life and spiritual world. Murshid dominates many Jiao Fangs (communities of his followers) and designates Ra'is and Akhund (Imam) to be in charge of mosques.

2. Building mausoleums for the founder, his successors, family members and outstanding disciples. After the founder and successors of a Menhuan pass away, the followers build mausoleums for them; sometimes they also build mausoleums for the missionaries from Arabia or Central Asia who were related

to their Menhuan. Thereby mausoleums have become a religious symbol for Menhuan.

3. Having strict and systematic Silsilah, a system of succession to murshid authority. Every Menhuan has built up its succession lineage which is called Silsilah in consideration of its development. Three types of succession are applied: by descendants, by clan members or by person of virtue. All Menhuans attach great importance to Silsilah, about which there are many mysterious legends.

4. Attaching importance to Tariqah, religious austerity. Tariqah is classified into three levels: Shari'ah, the lowest level, is of the basic conducts based on the "Six Beliefs" and "Five Pillars"; Tariqah, the mid level, is of the various austerities of Sufism; Haqiqah, the highest level, is of the highest spiritual state in which one gives up all the secular desires and reaches a state where one has been combined with the Creator. All Menhuans practice austerities in their own ways, and have absorbed elements from Confucianism, Buddhism and Taoism to some extent as well. Almost all Menhuans attach great importance to chanting Dhikr (praise to Allah), whilst different Menhuan chant differently and put on a mysterious appearance.

Menhuans are different from each other on administration.

◎ Arabic School in Urumchi, Xinjiang.

Generally speaking, they all practice a three-level administrative system: Murshid-Ra'is-Akhund. Murshid is the highest leader of all the followers both in spiritual and secular life, enjoying the supreme status and respect. Ra'is is the deputy or representative of the murshid dispatched to other places to administrate religious affairs. Only the murshid has the right to appoint Ra'is; even hereditary Ra'is must be authorized and conferred by the murshid. The basic unit of the Menhuan is Jiao Fang, and each Jiao Fang has a mosque and in each mosque there is an Akhund (Imam) who is in charge of the religious services and affairs of the Jiao Fang. Frankly speaking, Menhuan system is a feudal patriarchal clan system in nature born from the development of Islamic sects in China and characterized by religious worship, oppression and exploitation.

3. Mosque Education and Initiation of Nationalization of Islam in China

From the time Islam was introduced into China to the middle of the Ming Dynasty (1368-1644 A.D.), the Chinese Muslims' religious education had always been conducted in individual families by way of oral instruction by the elder generation. However, this method of education was restricted to a small range, lacking in organization and system, whose educational and social effects were not enough to meet the actual needs of the development of Islam in China. As time went on, Muslims in China adopted the Chinese language and gave up their mother tongue, leading to the loss of their ability to read scriptures in Arabic or Persian. However, no Chinese versions of Islamic scriptures had appeared yet. As a result, family education did not work efficiently any longer. Islam was faced with decline and Muslims became indifferent to their faith and religious life. Furthermore, rationalistic Confucian philosophy prevailed in the late period of the Ming Dynasty. Islam was in serious crises to exist and develop in China.

In this situation, the men of insight among the Hui Muslims began to explore ways to revitalize Islam, calling for developing Islamic education. Based on its development in the Yuan and Ming dynasties, the Huis had already shaped their national economic structure with agriculture as the core and commerce and animal husbandry as sideline industries. They were self-sufficient economically and lived a stable life. This made it possible for the development of Mosque education. The initiator of Mosque Education was Hu Dengzhou who lived in Weicheng, a town in Xianyang, Shaanxi Province in the period of Jia Jing (1522-1566 A.D.) and Wan Li (1573-1620 A.D.) of the Ming Dynasty. Weicheng is located to the west of Shaaxi where the Huis were concentrated. The Huis' economy here was comparatively developed, and they were in a better geographical position. At first Hu Dengzhou recruited students and taught them by himself in his family. Afterwards Lanzhou Ma, his second-generation student, moved the class to a mosque, marking the beginning of Mosque Education in China. Since Hu Dengzhou initiated Mosque Education, it began to rise throughout those places where Huis were concentrated, such as Shangdong, Zhejiang, Hunan, Hubei, Yunnan and Guangxi.

The purpose of Mosque Education was to find out and carry forward the righteousness of Islam and foster qualified Islamic personnel with orthodox thoughts of Sunni. This allowed Islamic education to be taught in an organized and systematic method instead of in individual families.

As Mosque Education developed, a comparatively complete educational system and a unified teaching method were gradually

◎ New built Pudong Mosque in Shanghai.

worked out. In its initial period, Mosque Education was not classified into higher or primary learning. It operated just as a private school did. It was conducted in mosques and Muslims invited an Imam to teach Islamic scriptures and religious knowledge to foster Islamic professionals. As it became more and more popular, and required by actual needs, Mosque Education developed towards specialization with the separation of higher learning from primary learning, and was classified into three levels: college, secondary school and primary school. College level was specialized to educate new Imam. The students at this level were called Khalifah or Manla. They were taught Arabic, Persian, Islamic Laws, doctrine, Qur'anic annotation and literature in a systematic way. Colleges were set up in large or medium-size mosques. The teachers of college were specially invited Imams, who were respectfully called Jingshi (master of scriptures), Mingjing (one who masters scriptures), Akhund (Imam), or Usta (sir). Secondary school level was a transitional link of Mosque Education. Generally secondary school level did not exist independently; it was either attached to primary school as its higher class or to college as its elementary class. Primary school level was the initial period of Mosque Education where Muslims could acquire basic Islamic knowledge. The main task of primary school was to teach Arabic letters, al-Kalimah al Tayibah (Testimony), Du'as used in daily prayers, and also teach how to perform and receive ablution, prayer and fast, and allow students to learn and recite Khatam (selected verses from the Holy Qur'an). There were no textbooks for primary school level, and it was taught by way of oral teaching. Of all the three levels of Mosque Education, the primary level was the most popular. In some places such as Shaanxi, Gansu, Ningxia and Qinghai, the primary Mosque Education was taken as compulsory. It was a duty of every parent to send their school-age children to primary school to receive basic Islamic education. The popularization of the primary level of Mosque Education was of great importance to the spread and development of Islam in China. In the past several hundred years, it was one of the major reasons why the Huis and other Muslim peoples could adhere to their Islamic faith.

In the early period of Mosque Education, it was compulsory for the students to transcribe the textbooks and the scriptures that the teachers used. It not only guaranteed Mosque Education to move forward smoothly, but also promoted the development of the Huis' Islamic calligraphy art, which developed into a unique branch of traditional calligraphic art in China.

Mosque Education was conducted in the unique language of Jingtang Yu (Yu means language. Mosque Education is called Jingtang Education in Chinese, so the language it uses is called Jingtang Yu). Jingtang Yu is a special expression that organizes Chinese, Arabic and Persian words and phrases in Chinese grammar. It is a special language with unique characteristics that was created by the Chinese Islamic scholars in specific historical and cultural circumstances to develop Islam in China, which is still in use in Mosque Education today.

The rise of Mosque Education gave the Huis and other Muslim peoples a systematic Islamic educational system and made Islam stride forwards towards a systemized and theorized religion. It was also the first popularization of Islamic scriptures, doctrine and thoughts, marking the beginning of the profound combination and extensive exchange of Sino-Arab cultures. Mosque Education brought up a great number of capable persons who devoted themselves into Islamic cause and education, fostered many well-known Islamic scholars, and put an end to the history that Islam was passed onto the next generation only by the elder generation's oral instruction. It initiated the movement of translating and writing scriptures in Chinese, and changed the situation that the Muslims in China were short of Chinese versions

◎ Eidkah Mosque in Kashgar, Xinjiang.

of Islamic scriptures and the true spirit of Islam could not be rightly interpreted. It brought the mosque's educational function into play in addition to its religious function. Mosque Education also helped to strengthen the contacts and exchanges among Jiao

Fangs, especially among the Islamic intellectuals, and enhanced the Islamic consciousness of other Muslims and improved their religious conduct.

The main centers of Mosque Education were Shaanxi, Shandong and Yunnan. Nanjing was one of the centers of Mosque Education as well, and it is here that the movement of translating and writing scriptures in Chinese was initiated.

4. Movement of Translating and Writing Scriptures in Chinese and Nationalization of Islam in China

During the transitional period between the Ming and Qing dynasties (the 17th century), following Mosque Education, the movement of translating and writing scriptures in Chinese rose vigorously. As all the translators and writers appeared in this period were well versed in four major religions, Confucianism, Buddhism, Taoism and Islam, and they preferred to expound Islamic doctrine in Confucian ways of thinking, so it was also called the movement of expounding scriptures with Confucianism.

The movement of translating and writing scriptures in Chinese was divided into three stages which started from Wang Daiyu, Muslim scholar in the transitional period between the Ming and Qing dynasties, and ended with Ma Lianyuan, Muslim scholar at the end of the Qing Dynasty, lasting over two hundred years. In this period of time there emerged a great number of

◎ The books and scriptures that the China Islamic Association has published in recent years.

well-known Islamic scholars emerged a great number of well-known Islamic scholars and Islamic works in Chinese that exerted a long-lasting influence upon Chinese Muslims and laid a solid theoretic foundation for the nationalization of Islam in China.

The first stage of the movement began with the publication of Wang Daiyu's "Expounding Islam", right up to the completion of Wu Zunqi's "Road Leading to Islam". In this period of time, the area around Nanjing and Jiangsu was the center of the movement, and the subject matter was always closely related to Mosque Education and Ilm al-Kalam (theology). The works of this period were either reading books for Mosque Education or a monograph to a theory, which were also read by intellectuals of other religions who wanted to know more about Islam. As a matter of fact, all these works borrowed something more or less from Confucianism and Buddhism, but their Islamic nature was still obviously demonstrated by their arguing and debating with Buddhism and Taoism, and criticizing certain views of Confucianism.

The representative figures of this period and their works are: Wang Daiyu, with his "Expounding Islam", "Islamic Great Learning" and "Right Answers to Truth-Seekers"; Zhang Zhong, with his "General Knowledge of Islam", "Essentials of Islam in Four Volumes"; Wu Zunqi, with his "An Introduction to Shariah" and "Road Leading to Islam". Furthermore, there were some others of great fame who translated many scriptures into Chinese, such as Ma Minglong with his "To Know Oneself and Wake up to Reality", Ma Junshi with his "Summary to Islamic History in Arabia", She Yunshan with his "Zhao Yuan Mi Jue", "Necessary Islamic Knowledge", and "Tui Yuan Zheng Da". All these works were prepared for those who were versed in Confucianism to study Islamic theology, and were also useful for ordinary Muslims to study Islamic doctrine.

The second stage of the movement of translating and writing scriptures into Chinese began from the time Ma Zhu translated his "Islamic Guidebook" to the time when Jin Tianzhu finished his "Answers to Doubts on Islam". The movement was pushed to its peak in this period by intellectuals and their works with

Liu Zhi as the most outstanding one. The movement also extended to other places, not only being limited in the area around Nanjing and Suzhou any more. The mainstream of the movement came to be connected closely with Confucian thoughts. The object of the movement was turned to the outside spheres of Islam, hoping to eliminate others religions' doubts of Islam and gain understanding and support from the feudal ruling class and scholar-officials. Thus, the audience and object of the movement changed from those either illiterate or those who only read Islamic scriptures to those who were well versed in the three religions. As a result, the pure Islamic nature of the translated and written works was not in existence any more, and was replaced by a form of obvious combination of Islam with Confucianism, which presented dual characteristics of both religions. The Islamic scholars in this period stopped criticizing Confucian thoughts but emphasized the common ground between Islam and Confucianism, advocating learning both Islam and Confucianism.

The representative figures of this period and their works are: Ma Zhu, with his "Islamic Guidebook"; Liu Zhi, with his "Arabian Principles of Nature", "Arabian Ceremonies", "Life of the Greatest Prophet of All"; Jin Tianzhu, with his "Answers to Doubts on Islam"; Ma Boliang, with his "A Sketch of Islamic

Law"; Mi Wanji, with his "Thoughts on Islamic Institutions". Among all the works mentioned above, the ones by Liu Zhi were of the greatest influence, being considered as the representative works that pushed the movement of expounding Islam with Confucian thoughts to the peak. His "Arabian Ceremonies" was cataloged in "Complete Collection in Four Treasuries" as the only Islamic book selected, being thought highly by scholars of both the Huis and the Hans.

As the social situation changed, the third stage of the

movement of translating and writing scriptures in Chinese took on new characteristics different from the first two stages.

As colonial powers invaded in 1840, China was reduced to a semi-colony; traditional Confucian thought and culture was greatly impacted. The failures of two uprisings of the Huis and the two cases of literary inquisition related to Islam halted the movement of translating and writing scriptures in Chinese for dozens of years. The center of the movement was transferred to Yunnan, and the subject was expanded to astronomy, geography, literature and Qur'an translation from theology, religious philosophy, religious system and doctrine, becoming much more extensive. The content of the translating and writing came to focus on propagandizing Islamic theory on the hereafter, mysticism and the thoughts on nourishing one's inborn nature. This was much more closely related to Confucianism.

The representative figures of this period and their works are: Ma Dexin, with his "Ending of Creation", "Concise Four-Aspect Exposition of Islam", "Guide to Healthy Life", "What Islam Is" and "Explanations to Prayers"; Ma Lianyuan, with his "Annals of Truth", Lan Xu, with his "Right Learning of Arabia". The revised and enlarged edition of "Answers to Doubts on Islam" was completed in this period, too. "Islamic Way" appeared in this period and was of special value for it sketched out Dhikr, one of the major courses practiced by mystics in Islam. As the third stage concluded, the whole movement of translating and writing scriptures in Chinese that pursued the combination of Islamic with Confucian thoughts and cultures came to an end.

The movement of expounding scriptures with Confucianism excrted great influence upon Islam in China and made a tremendous contribution to its development. Since Du Huan wrote a brief introduction to Islam in Chinese in his "Jing Xing Ji" (Where I Traveled) in the Tang Dynasty for the first time, a few scholars, both Hui and Non-Hui, also touched Islam and tried to interpret its doctrine within the terms of Confucianism, Buddhism and Taoism. However, they only provided very simple information on Islam, far from being enough. With the strenuous efforts of Hui scholars for generations, starting from Wang Daiyu, tremendous accomplishments were achieved in the movement of translating and writing scriptures in Chinese. Using Confucian terms and thoughts, they made profound studies on Islamic doctrine, leading to the breaking of the estrangement between Islam and Confucianism, Buddhism and Taoism in the sphere of ideology. By absorbing the thoughts of other religions, Islamic doctrine and philosophy was broadened and the influence of Islam in China was enlarged as well. The long-lasting situation of tripartite confrontation of Confucianism, Buddhism and Taoism came to an end as a result and a new sphere of ideology was opened in China. The Islamic philosophy on human nature and rationality was combined with that of Confucianism in the movement of translating and writing scriptures in Chinese, which enriched the content of this sphere in the history of Chinese ideology.

5. Combination of Islam with Traditional Chinese Culture

The movement of translating and writing scriptures in Chinese that occurred in the middle of the 17th century accclerated the process of the nationalization of Islam in China, making Islam, a religion coming from the outside world, not only root deeply in China, but also amalgamated with traditional Chinese culture, for Islam in China by then had taken on obvious characteristics of traditional Chinese culture, whether in the form of presentation or deep-seated doctrine and ethics.

Firstly, Islam in China has been influenced more or less by

© Grand Mosque of Cangzhou, Hebei.

◎ Huajuexiang Mosque in Xi'an .

the traditional Chinese culture on aspects of architecture, festivals and customs. Almost all the mosques in Arab and Islamic countries in central Asia have domes on the roofs and minarets for observing the moon and calling for prayers. But in China, except a few ancient mosques in coastal area and in Xinjiang such as the Guang Ta Mosque in Guangzhou, the Qing Jing Mosque in Quanzhou and the Eidkah Mosque in Kashgar that were constructed with Arab and Central Asian architecture, most of the mosques in the inland, such as the Hua Jue Xiang Mosque in Xi'an, the Jing Jue Mosque in Nanjing, the Niu Jie Mosque and the Dong Si Mosque in Beijing, the Qiao Men Mosque in

Lanzhou, the Nan Guan Mosque in Linxia, the Southern Mosque in Jinan and the Souther Mosque in Cangzhou, all adopted traditional Chinese architecture, which is a temple-like compound with buildings around a square courtyard, and a screen wall facing the gate. The construction inside the mosque was richly ornamented with pillars and beams carved and painted, and also decorated with horizontal inscribed boards and antithetical couplets. For instance, there are four Chinese characters inscribed on the ridge of the Jing Jue Mosque: Wu Xiang Bao Dian (temple without idols), displaying unique Chinese Islamic architecture.

As for religious festivals, Chinese Muslims, as with other Muslims around the world, regard the three traditional Islamic festivals, namely 'Id al-Fitr (fast-breaking festival), 'Id al-Azha (festival of sacrifice) and Mawlid al-Nabiy (birthday of the Prophet Muhammad and also the day when he passed away), as the most important festivals. However, in some places in China, Muslims also call 'Id al-Azha "Festival of Fidelity". Just from the naming of the festival we can see that it has taken on Chinese characteristic. Usually in foreign countries, Mawlid al-Nabiy (March 12th A.H., both the birthday of the Prophet Muhammad and the day when he passed away) is a day when Muslims get together to celebrate the birthday of the Prophet Muhammad,

◎ Muslims celebrating 'Id al-Kurban.

and commemorate him by reciting the Holy Qur'an and narrating the story of his life. However, Chinese Muslims celebrate it on any day of March A.H., not just March 12th. In doing so, they also commemorate the anniversary of the death of their ancestors, reciting the Holy Qur'an and slaughtering sheep or cattle to dine together to show their condolence. In fact, they celebrate this festival as the Anniversary of the Prophet's Demise. Besides the above three festivals, the Chinese Muslims also attach importance to Ashura and the Anniversary of Fatimah's Demise. Ashura is on January 10th A.H., being the day to commemorate the occasions when Prophet Adam, Prophet Ibrahim and Prophet Nuh were rescued from danger. In some places in China, Muslims also call this the "Festival of Porridge", believing that Prophet Nuh relieved the human race with the last porridge made of beans after floating in the flood for six months, so men after him commemorate it by eating porridge on this day. The way they celebrate this festival and the story they tell concerning it is different from that in foreign countries. Anniversary of Fatimah's Demise is on June 15th A.H., being the day to commemorate the demise of Fatimah, daughter of Prophet Muhammad and wife of Ali. Chinese Muslims respect Fatimah far more than they respect Khadija, wife of the Prophet. This is also different from what foreign Muslims do. In addition, some Muslims in the Northwest worship the murshids (guides) and saints of their sect or Menhua, and hold ceremonies to commemorate the anniversary of their demise, just as they celebrate Mawlid al-Nabiy. Sometimes there are several thousand followers getting together for the ceremony, quite a rare phenomenon abroad.

In respect of religious customs, only on few points such as taboo with food are Chinese Muslims completely in accordance with foreign Muslims, and on other aspects such as language, name, dress, wedding and funeral they have taken on the features of Chinese habits and customs. Chinese Muslims use Arabic or Persian words and expressions only in religious services, but speak Chinese during ordinary times. Their dress has evolved to be similar with that of the Hans. They use Chinese name, and will be given an Islamic name (selected from the names of prophets, saints or noble persons) at birth by an Imam, or sometimes combine Chinese name and Islamic name together to be their full name. As for the custom on marriage, they often invite an Imam to preside over the celebrations and celebrate it by playing the flute and trumpet as the Hans do. Of course it is not in line with the teaching of Islam that music is prohibited on the wedding except drumming. Chinese Muslims always practice a rapid and simple funeral (the deceased must be buried within three days with the body

◎ A wedding banquet of the Uighurs.

only covered with white cloth, no cerements or any burial articles) as is required by Islamic Law, and invite an Imam to recite the Holy Qur'an. On the other hand, Muslims in certain places in China show their condolence to the deceased by wearing mourning apparel, ornamenting the tomb, and commemorating the 7th day, the 40th day, the hundredth day, one-year anniversary and three-year anniversary. Obviously they have been influenced by Chinese traditions and customs on this aspect.

Secondly, in respect of deep-seated doctrine and ethics, Muslims in China adhere to the fundamental belief of Islam and the basic principles of the Holy Qur'an and Hadith on the one hand, and have absorbed others from traditional Chinese cultural ingredients including Confucian, Taoist and Buddhist thoughts, and integrated them with Islam organically, making it more systemized and theorized, turning Islamic doctrine and ethical thoughts into one with Chinese characteristics on the other hand.

Believing in the Oneness of the Creator is the fundamental belief of Islam, without which one deviates from Islam. The Muslim scholars, who appeared in the transitional period between Ming and Qing dynasties with Wang Daiyu and Liu Zhi as representative, integrated the Islamic doctrine on the Oneness of the Creator with the Confucian theory of the Supreme Ultimate.

◎　A table plaque on which al-Kalimah al-Tayibah (Testimony) was carved, produced in the Ming Dynasty and reserved in Dongsi Mosque, Beijing.

On the one hand, they accepted the viewpoint of the Supreme Ultimate theory that all things in the universe originated from five elements (metal, wood, water, fire and earth); the five elements originated from Yin and Yang (two opposing principles in nature, the former feminine and negative, the latter masculine and positive), and Yin and Yang originated from the Supreme Ultimate which originated from nothing. On the other hand, they asserted that there already exists a creator before nothing; it is Allah, who created the world and all the things in it. Thus, they both affirmed the fundamental belief of Islam that "there is no God but Allah", and integrated it with Confucian thoughts. Another example is how they dealt with the relations between the faith to Allah and the loyalty to ruler. In the Islamic point of view, the faith to Allah should not be shaken even a bit, but this is contrary to Confucian thought. To coordinate the relations between the two, the Chinese Islamic scholar asserted that being loyal only to ruler and father, but not to Allah, was not true loyalty, and being faithful only to Allah, but not to ruler and father, was not true faith; being faithful to Allah, loyal to ruler and obedient to parents were three virtues that one should pursue throughout life. It is in this way that they successfully settled the problem of how to coordinate the relations between faith to Allah and loyalty to ruler of a country where Islam was not the state religion.

In respect of ethics, Chinese Islamic scholars ingeniously integrated the basic principles of the Holy Qur'an and Hadith with the ethical thoughts of Confucianism, making both tally with the ethical thoughts of Confucianism, and not deviating from the fundament principles of Islam, building up the unique ethical thought system of Chinese Islam as a result. Among all the Islamic scholars who appeared in the transitional period between Ming and Qing dynasties Liu Zhi was the one who synthesized this system of thought and brought it to its highest development. In his "Arabian Ceremonies", he gave wide coverage to expounding his theory of "Five Human Relations". The "Five Human

Relations" actually means the ethical relationship of five aspects: ruler with subject, father with son, husband with wife, and one with friends. To integrate it, which is the kernel of traditional Confucian ethics and the foundation stone of the feudal idea of the "Three Cardinal Guides and Five Constant Virtues", with Chinese Islamic ethics, Liu Zhi arranged the consecution of the "Five Human Relations" in Islamic order with "Allah being the Creator" as starting-point. He believed that Allah had created the world and all things in it, and the primogenitor of human beings, Adam and Hawwa (Eve in the Bible) as well, through whom human beings originated. Allah also created the five human relations and took it as the foundation of all virtues to perfect His creation of human beings. Liu Zhi arranged the "Five Human Relations" not in the order of traditional Confucian ethical thought as "Three Cardinal Guides and Five Constant Virtues". He placed the relationship between husband and wife above all the rest, believing that it was the foundation of all human relations. Only by dealing with it well can the family be managed well; only by managing the family well can each one be placed in the right position, can the country be administered properly, and can relatives and friends be tied closely. Here he took the positive Confucian ethical thought, namely "cultivating one's moral character, putting one's house in order, running the country well, and letting peace prevail on earth", as the basis for arranging the order of human relations. The reason why he did so was just to make it tally with the tradition of Chinese feudal ethics. Simply due to the above reason, Liu Zhi believed that marriage was the foundation of human beings (the five human relations started from marriage); brotherhood was the basis of love (the love of human being started from brotherhood); friendship was the foundation to achieve virtue (it could help achieve the other four human relations). He also believed that the order of the Five Human Relations as well as the reasoning within them was created by Allah. Islam set up Five Pillars to carry out the Divine Laws, and Five Human Relations to carry out the Human Laws. The Divine Laws and the Human Laws covered one another and could not be separated. Carrying out the Human Laws laid the foundation for the Divine Laws, while carrying out the Divine Laws pointed one in the right direction to the Human Laws. Only fulfilling both the Divine Laws and the Human Laws could one complete what one should do as a man. The "Divine Laws" actually refer to the laws and truth set by Allah, it was a term that Liu Zhi borrowed from Confucianism to expound Islamic ethic. Thus, starting from Allah and concluding with the Five Human

◎ A old Uighur man and a kid.

Relations set by Allah, the system of Chinese Islamic ethics was finally established.

Liu Zhi adhered to two basic principles when he expounded the Five Human Relations: firstly, to absorb all the Confucian ethical thoughts that were not contrary to basic Islamic principles without any changes, and quote a great deal of the Holy Qur'an and Hadith to prove them, and try his best to expound them in an Islamic point of view; secondly, to evade ingeniously the Confucian ethical thoughts that were contrary to basic Islamic principles, or give them new explanation to make them in line with both the tradition of Confucian ethic and the basic principles of Islam. In respect of the relationship between husband and wife, Liu Zhi maintained that husband should love wife and wife should respect husband; husband should instruct wife to know and abide by the doctrine and laws of Islam, and maintain her with legal income, while wife should be obedient to husband as respect. In respect of the relation between father and son, he advocated that father should be kind to son and son should be filial towards father, emphasizing that parents give birth to children on behalf of Allah, so they should fulfill their duty to raise them, treat them with kindness from the time they are conceived to the time they marry, and children should be grateful to Allah and their parents for their birth and up-bring, and respect and care for them to fulfill their filial duty. In respect of the relation between ruler and subject, Liu Zhi held that a ruler should be benevolent to his subject and the subject should be loyal to his ruler, emphasizing that a ruler should take it as their first duty to observe and understand Allah, for Allah is the greatest example of benevolence, also learning from prophets, for they are the ones spreading Allah's laws and are can act as his model. A subject should take loyalty as the criteria in carrying out his duty, for the power of ruler is divinely authorized. Ruler is the reflection of Allah, so subject should be loyal to ruler so as to show his faith to Allah. In respect of the relation between brothers, he advocated that the elder should be tolerant to the younger and the younger should be courteous to the elder, emphasizing that brothers are like hands, while the elder is like the right hand above the younger and the younger is like the left hand below the elder (it is thought that right is above left in Islam); they are distinguished by age but tied closely by blood. In respect of the relation between friends, he advocated that they should be both loyal and honest to each other, only by being loyal and honest and virtuous can one be a helpful friend. Only by being associated with a helpful friend can one be virtuous in this world and be rescued from disaster in the Hereafter, and accomplish happiness in both worlds. Although Liu Zhi used Confucian terms in expounding his theory of Five Human Relations, he adhered to basic Islamic principles, repeatedly elucidating ethical thoughts initiated in the Holy Qur'an as worshiping Allah, being just, preserving one's purity, doing good, keeping to one's promise and being tolerant. As for the ideas of "keeping chastity"" and "worshiping ancestors", which are of great importance in Confucian ethic, he avoided making any comment. According to Confucian ethics, a widow who remains unmarried after the death of her husband deserves high admiration. Zhu Xi, a representative Confucian, even proclaimed that it is a minor thing to be starved to death, while it is a big thing to lose chastity, advocating that the woman who can remain unmarried after the death of her husband should be cited and a memorial archway

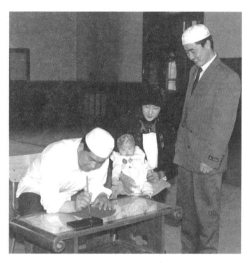

© Imam giving a newborn baby an Islamic name.

should be built for her chastity, while the one who can not do so should be punished. However, it is contrary to the principle indicated in the Holy Qur'an that a widow can remarried if she wants to do so, so Liu Zhi did not make any comment on this aspect. As for those of the Confucian ethical viewpoints that can't be avoided but contrary to the basic principles of Islam, he gave new explanations. For instance, in respect of the relationship between ruler and subject, the Confucian ethic calls for blind devotion to ruler, it has been even developed to the point that a subject has to die if his ruler wants him to do so. It is obviously contrary to the Islamic thought that faith in Allah cannot be shaken even a bit. So in the chapter "Ruler", Liu Zhi made it clear by quoting the Qur'anic verse that Allah ordered Dawud to be the ruler of the world: first, the power of the ruler is authorized by Allah; second, Allah orders the ruler to be wise and able, otherwise he will be punished. Restrained by the above two points, the contradiction between loyalty to ruler and faith to Allah was settled. In his point of view, the ruler is the king who has a visible body, while Allah is the imageless dominator. Praising Allah is the noblest of divine work, while serving a ruler is the noblest of human work. Only when praising Allah and serving ruler are both done well, can the divine work and human work be coordinated.

To sum it up, the integration of Islam with traditional Chinese culture, especially on deep-seated aspects such as those of doctrine and ethics, accelerated the nationalization of Islam in China, and characterized it with unique national features and made it different from that of other countries and regions. Confucian ideology had always occupied the dominant position in Chinese feudal society. Rulers used it as a tool to run the country, and people were influenced and restricted by it. Any ideology that is not in line with Confucianism could not find a place in China to root and grow. Chinese Islam positively adapted itself to the Confucian ideology, the kernel of the traditional

Chinese culture, and used Confucian terms to expound its own doctrine. That was of great importance for Muslims living in China to learn about Islam, and also for Islam itself to exist and develop in China. Although Islam in China has been branded many aspects of the native nation, its fundamentals such as the "Six Beliefs", "Five Pillars" and various food taboos remain unchanged. Simply due to this, Chinese Muslims have earned the respect of foreign Muslims, and have always been in good relation with them.

· ·

© Prayer hall of the Ningxia Islamic Institute.

CHAPTER 3
ISLAM IN THE REPUBLIC OF CHINA PERIOD

In 1911, the Qing Dynasty was overthrown in the Revolution of 1911, and China stepped into a new era---the Republic Period. In this short period of time lasting only 40 years, gigantic changes took place in China on aspects of social politics, economy and culture. As the autocratic monarchy was overthrown, the bureaucratic apparatus, imperial examination system and ceremonies and proprieties associated with it were all abolished. China started to transit from a semi-colony to a modern new society. It was a time of turmoil for China, beset by internal disturbance and foreign aggression. It was also a time when revolutionary movements rose one after another. Having gotten rid of the high-handed ruling Qing government, and motivated by revolutionary thought, Chinese Muslims walked out of a blocked situation, and recovered and built up their national consciousness. They began to consider changes on various aspects such as equality of political status, improvement of economy, development of education and freedom of religious belief. As a result, a new Islamic cultural movement was initiated by the Muslim scholars who were both well versed in religion and had a modern mind.

1. Rise of New Islamic Schools and Muslim Organizations

1). BIRTH OF NEW ISLAMIC SCHOOLS

Around the Revolution of 1911, motivated by bourgeois democratic thought, Hui Muslims in inland China were active in cultural movement, religious reform and educational development, attempting to adapt Chinese Islam to the new historic trend. Many well-known figures within Islamic circles connected the fortune of the state with that of their nation and religion, placing "loving and defending the motherland" above all others. For example, Ding Zhuyuan, an advanced Chinese Muslim, proclaimed: "To defend the state is to defend Islam; to love the state is to love oneself"; "No matter which religion one follows, being a Chinese citizen, one should endeavor together with others for the fortune of our country. Could the religion survive if the country collapsed?" They also proposed strengthening the unity of the Huis with the Hans, saying that they should adhere to their own religions while respect the other's

115

◎ Old Imams and young generation Imams.

freedom of religious belief. Confronted by the actual situation that very few Muslims were literate, and many people knew little about Islam, they pointed out that only when both the economy and education of the Huis was developed could Islam show its charm. With their motivation and efforts, new Muslim schools sprang up like mushrooms all over the country where Muslims were concentrated. The reason why they were called "new schools" was that they differed essentially from traditional Islamic education. In these schools, natural and social sciences such as geography, maths, physics and chemistry were taken as major courses just as other ordinary schools had done, while they offered courses on religion as well, which was the continuity of traditional

Islamic education. The educational objective of the new schools was not only to foster capable persons for Islamic causes but also to cultivate useful persons for society. Thus the students that the new schools had educated were scattered in all walks of life, not only confined to Islamic circles. Though some of the new schools were established in mosques or run by mosques, the method by which they were run had made them socialized, exerting a positive influence upon all circles.

From the time Tong Cong, a well-known Muslim in Zhenjiang, Jiangsu, established "Mu Yuan School" in 1906, Muslim primary schools rose one after another all over the country, among which the eminent ones were mostly run by well-known Islamic educationalists, such as Jingshi (now Beijing) Muslim Bi-Level (primary and secondary) School run by Wan Kuan at the Niujie Mosque in 1908, the "Xie Jin Primary School" run by educationalist Ma Linyi in Shaoyang, Hunan, in 1906. At the same time, Muslims came to realize the importance of the new type of education at secondary level, and set up a number of secondary and normal schools, such as Muslim Secondary School (renamed as Northwest Public School later) established in 1928, Mu Xing Secondary School run by Sun Zhongwei and others in Hangzhou in 1928, Ming De Secondary School run by Yang

Wenbo and others in Kunming in 1930, Crescent Woman's Secondary School initiated collectively by Yang Xinmin, Chen Yongxiang, Zhao Zhenwu, Ma Songting, Wang Mengyang and others in Beijing in 1935. The normal schools established in this period of time are: Shanghai Islamic Normal School, Wanxian Islamic Normal School in Sichuan, and Yunting Normal School in Ningxia, which was the first public Islamic normal school in China. Among all the schools established in this period of time, Chengda Normal School is worth mentioning most. Chengda, the name of the school, indicates fostering character and ability. It obliged itself to cultivate qualified teachers, enlighten the Huis

◎ The Xinjiang Islamic Institute.

with knowledge, develop Islamic culture, and undertake to train school masters, Imams and leaders of Muslim organizations. To foster qualified teachers who were well versed in both Islamic knowledge and Chinese culture, in addition to the major courses on Islam, the school also offered courses on Chinese language, Chinese history

© The students of the Beijing Islamic Institute are in the parade celebrating the 50th anniversary of the People's Republic of China.

and geography, natural sciences, pedagogy and psychology to train the students to read Islamic scriptures in Arabic and understand the Holy Qur'an and Hadith comprehensively, and make allow them to acquire the ability to study Islamic philosophy, laws, ethics and history. In 1932, the first group of students graduated from Chengda, among whom some were sent to Azhar University in Egypt for further study, being the first group of students abroad in the history of Chinese Islam. Chengda Normal School practiced a schoolmaster responsibility system under the leadership of the board of trustees. It was a typical new type of Islamic school in the modern era of China, which played an important role in Chinese Islamic education and modern Arabic teaching. When the People's Republic of China was funded in 1949, Chengda Normal School was merged with Northwest Public School into Hui Min College, the first institution of higher learning for the Huis in China.

2). MUSLIM ORGANIZATIONS AND THEIR ACTIVITIES

During the period between the end of the Qing Dynasty and beginning of the Republic (the early 20th century), motivated by the thought of "saving the country, saving the nation and saving Islam", a group of Muslim intellectuals educated in new schools were active in initiating nation-wide or local Islamic organizations. These organizations were different from ordinary ones because they were not involved directly in religious services, but acted as a media in strengthening the contact and unity of the Muslims, promoting academic studies on Islam, and carrying on activities of saving the country and Islam. They engendered considerable social effects.

◎ The China Islamic Association published a great number of Islamic books and scriptures, which aroused Muslim youths' enthusiasm for learning.

a). Cultural Groups and Organizations

The China Muslim Association for Common Progress initiated by Wang Kuan, Hou Deshan and others in Beijing in 1912 was one of the representative organizations of this kind, which pursued "uniting the Huis at home, developing Islam, promoting the Huis' education and improving the Huis welfare". By 1936, it had set up more than 200 branches in almost all provinces, and became a nongovernmental Hui cultural organization enjoying the greatest fame and widest coverage within China at the time. It was active in launching various activities, such as inviting Wang Jingzhai, a well-known Imam, to translate the Holy Qur'an, running Muslim primary and secondary schools and Arabic school, universalizing education for the Huis, running factories to improve Hui life, and developing charities. As its members were mostly Hui officials, businessmen and Imams, this organization exerted a considerable influence on Hui Muslims.

In addition, there were other organizations such as the China Huis' Council in Beijing, which was a nongovernmental organization that appeared first and was named after the Huis, and the China Islamic Cultural Association in Shanghai.

b). Academic Groups and Organizations

The Islamic Society, established by the students of Jingshi Muslim Bi-Level School in 1917, took as its objectives to pursue academic studies and expound Islamic doctrine. Any Muslim adults capable of study could join the Society. It was one of many academic organizations in the modern history of Chinese Islam. Besides, there were other organizations such as the China Islamic Society in Shanghai.

c). Religious Groups and Organizations

Among the religious groups and organizations the China Islamic Trade Council was of considerable influence, whose objectives were to develop Muslim brotherhood at home and abroad, improve the welfare of the Huis, unite all Muslims in China and assist the country. There were also other groups and organization of this kind such as the Islamic Federation of the Republic of China in Nanjing, the Tianjin Islamic Federation in Tianjin and the Chinese Muslim Cultural and Fraternal Association in Hong Kong.

d). Educational Groups and Organizations

Groups and organizations of this kind appearing then were: the Lanzhou Islamic Society for Encouraging Learning (renamed as the Gansu Provincial Islamic Education Promotion Council afterwards), the Ninghai Islamic Promotion Council in Qinghai (renamed as the Qinghai Islamic Promotion Council afterwards), the Changde Islamic Education Assistance Council in Hunan and the China Hui Education Promotion Council in Nanjing. The Changde Islamic Education Assistance Council in Hunan was typical among them, which devoted itself to reforming Mosque Education into one that offered courses on both Chinese and Arabic. It encouraged mosques to set up common primary

schools, and published various Islamic scriptures to provide reading material on Islamic knowledge for Muslims who could not read Arabic, such as the 12-volume Elementary Chinese Reader and 1-volume advanced Arabic Reader, both of which were bilingual in Arabic and Chinese.

e). Youths Groups and Organizations

The China Islamic Youth Society was funded in Nanjing, whose members were mostly Muslim youths who had received secondary or higher education. It was active in uniting Muslim youths to launch various academic activities on Islam. In Guangzhou, Taiyuan and Shenyang, there were organizations of this kind too. In addition, with the purpose to "unite the Hui women and expound Islam", He Wenyu, a young Hui woman in Shanghai, along with others established the Shanghai Muslim Women Association, and published "Muslim Women" magazine.

f). Charitable Groups and Organizations

The Guangdong Islamic Society for the Aged was a Muslim charitable organization that worked for mutual help among the aged of the Huis. Essentially as form of life insurance, it only took on religious features afterwards.

2. *Publishing Institutions and Islamic Publications*

As the new education movement kept developing, more and more Muslim organizations sprang up, and the publication of Islamic books and newspapers also stepped into a new era. Among the publishing institutions the following ones were of considerable influence:

1). PUBLISHING DIVISION OF CHENGDA NORMAL SCHOOL IN BEIJING

Chengda Normal School set up publishing division soon after it moved to Beijing. Almost every month there were new books published such as "Islam" by Na Zijia, "Studies on Chinese Islamic History" by Jin Jitang, "Islam and Life" by Ma Songting, "True Origin" by Ma Zicheng, "New Arabic Grammar" by Dr. Furfil from Egypt, and "Diaries Written in the Journey to the West" by Zhao Zhenwu,. It also photocopied a number of original Arabic scriptures, such as the Holy Qur'an (Othman edition). It

125

◎ The books and magazines that the China Islamic Association has published in recent years.

could cast Arabic letters itself, and published books in Arabic.

2). BEIPING (NOW BEIJING) ISLAMIC PUBLISHING HOUSE

Beiping Publishing House was previously entrusted to print scriptures and books in the name of Islamic Publishing House. As it developed further, it possessed the printing equipment of its own and began to print books and distribute them by itself, and the category of the scriptures and books it published broadened and the subscription increased as well. The scriptures and books it published were mainly the works translated or written by well-known scholars in the Ming and Qing dynasties.

3). JINCHENG BAOZHEN HOUSE

This was one of the most eminent nongovernmental publishing institutions specializing in publishing Islamic scriptures and books. A great number of well-known scriptures and works translated or written by Muslim scholars was published here, such as "The Essence of the Way to Allah", "Four Essays on Islam", "The True Explanation to the Right Religion", "The Great Learning of Islam", "Guide to Islam", "Arabian Ceremonies", "Arabian Thought", "Life of the Prophet Muhammad", ""More About Islamic Explanations", "Essence of Four Principles of Islam".

4). CHINA ISLAMIC SCRIPTURE BUREAU

The China Islamic Scripture Bureau was engaged mainly in distributing the Holy Qur'an, Hadith and other Islamic scriptures originally published by the Halbi Publishing House of Egypt. It also published various books itself, such as "Chinese-Arabic Bilingual Reader on Phonetics", "5-Volume Chinese-Arabic Bilingual Reader", "Chinese-Arabic Bilingual Questions and Answers on Six Islamic Beliefs", "Chinese-Arabic Bilingual Pamphlet on Prayer", "Chinese Version of the Selections from the Holy Qur'an", "Zhongshan Model Dialog", "Letter Origins",

"Preliminary Arabic Reader", "Advanced Arabic Reader" and "Textbook on Islamic Bath". In response to the request of readers, it reprinted many important works translated or written by well-known Muslim scholars during the movement of translating and writing scriptures in Chinese.

5). SHANGHAI MUSLIM SCRIPTURE SOCIETY

The Shanghai Muslim Scripture Society was engaged mainly in reprinting the Holy Qur'an, Hadith and various scriptures and books on Islamic doctrine, law, ethic, and Arabic grammar and rhetoric brought by Chinese pilgrims from Mecca. It also sold various magazines and newspapers in Chinese.

6). SHANGHAI ISLAMIC CULTURE SUPPLY SOCIETY

The Shanghai Islamic Culture Supply Society was an organization that engaged mainly in reprinting and distributing Islamic scriptures and books. It also offered help to Muslim scholars and Chinese pilgrims to Mecca.

Furthermore, since the beginning of the Republic Period in areas where Muslims were concentrated, publications concerning Islam sprang up like mushrooms. The major ones included:

a). Publications focusing on doctrines: "The China Islamic

Society Monthly" in Shanghai, "Islamic Journal" in Yunnan, "Arabian Knowledge" in Guangdong, "Zhenzong Journal" in Beijing and "Light of Islam" in Tianjin.

b). Publications focusing on religious culture: "Yue Hua Journal" in Beijing, "Rays of Dawn" and "Muslim Youth" in Nanjing, and "Human" in Shanghai.

c). Publications specialized in the religions in the frontiers: "Turk" and "Tianshan Mountain" in Nanjing.

d). School publications: "School Journal of Chengda Normal School" in Beijing, "Journal of China Islamic Youth Society" in Nanjing and "Islamic Students" in Shanghai.

Among all the above-mentioned publications, which were started in 1929 and stopped in 1949, "Islamic Journal" was the one that lasted the longest period (20 years) and had the largest subscription, being the most outstanding Islamic publication in the Republic Period.

3. Translation and Publication of the Holy Qur'an

In the 1,000 years since Islam was introduced into China in the 7th century up until the Ming Dynasty, there were no printed editions of the Holy Qur'an either in Arabic or in Chinese. Transcribing by hand was the only way to maintain and spread the Holy Qur'an. To learn it depended mainly on the oral teachings of the Imam, or one had to learn it in Arabic because by that time there had not appeared scholars who were well versed in both

◎ A handwritten Holy Qur'an transcribed 300 years ago and reversed in the library of the China Islamic Institute.

Arabic and Chinese and could translate the Holy Qur'an into Chinese, furthermore, the Holy Qur'an is a scripture revealed in Arabic, so it was afraid that to translate it into other languages would not deliver its real meaning and impact one's Iman (faith). As Islam developed in China, the Muslims in China who spoke Chinese hungered for explanation of the Holy Qur'an in Chinese. So Mosque Education rose, and Imams undertook to do it in Jingtang Yu, a mixed language of Chinese, Arabic and Persian used in Mosque Education. At the same time, some Imams and scholars who were well versed in Arabic attempted to translate the Holy Qur'an into Chinese. By the end of the Ming Dynasty and beginning of the Qing Dynasty (the 17th century), Islamic scholars translated the Qur'anic verses that were quoted in their works. By the middle and end of the 19th century, "Selections from the Holy Qur'an" translated by Ma Zhiben, and 5-volume "Literal Translation of the Holy Qur'an" by Ma Fuchu were published. As European language versions of the Holy Qur'an were transmitted into China and the New Culture Movement developed, it was taken into consideration to translate the entire Holy Qur'an into Chinese.

From the 1920's to the time when New China was founded, the complete Chinese versions of the Holy Qur'an were published

successively, among which the ones with greater influence were: 1) "Holy Qur'an" translated from Japanese by Li Tiezheng, a Non-Muslim, which was the earliest complete Chinese version of the Holy Qur'an published in Beijing in 1927; 2) "Chinese Translation of the Holy Qur'an" translated from English by Ji Juemi and others in Shanghai in 1931; 3) "Translation and Interpretation of the Holy Qur'an" edition A, B and C translated by Wang Jingzhai and published in 1932, 1943 and 1946 respectively; 4) "Additional Interpretation to Chinese Translation of the Holy Qur'an" done by Liu Jinbiao in Beijing in 1943; 5) "Essence of the Holy Qur'an" translated by Yang Jingxiu and published by Publishing Division of Chengda Normal School in Beijing in 1947. All these Chinese versions of the Holy Qur'an with different characteristics indicated the delightful progress on the work of translating the Holy Qur'an. They became more and more accurate in meaning and easier and easier to understand.

4. Chinese Muslims' Active Participation in the War of Resistance against Japan

After Japan launched the invasion war into China in 1937, under the leadership of the Chinese Communist Party, all Muslims from various peoples, with the Huis in particular, took an active part in the campaign of fighting against the Japanese invaders and saving the country. The Hui Detachment led by Ma Benzhai was a famous anti-Japanese military force organized spontaneously by the Chinese Muslims. Ma Benzhai was a colonel in the Army of the Northeast. When his hometown was ruined by Japanese, Ma Benzhai raised the standard of revolt against Japanese invasion in the Dongxin Zhuang Mosque, and was followed by many Hui youths. The Hui Detachment with Ma Benzhai himself as commander and Guo Lushun from the Red Army as commissar scored many victories with flexible guerilla tactics. His army soon expanded to 2300 people. Swearing to fight for the country and the people, and have the Japanese pay for their bloody crimes, the Hui Detachment fought in over 870 battles in 6 years, wiping

◎ Hui Detachment that was active during the Anti-Japan War.

out 36,700 people of the Japanese puppet army, capturing or destroying hundreds of blockhouses and fortified points, railways and bridges, seizing large quantities of firearms, ammunition, war horses and military supplies. For the bravery that the Hui soldiers had shown and the brilliant successes they had achieved, the Hui Detachment was called "iron army that can't be defeated". It left a glorious page in the history of the Chinese people's war of resistance.

The Hui military force initiated by Liu Geping, Wang Lianfang and other intellectuals in the south of Tianjin soon expanded to more than 400 people. Afterwards it was enlarged to be "the Hui Detachment in Hebei and Shandong Border Area", with Liu Zhenhuan as commander and Wang Lianfang as commissar. The Hui Detachment respected the habits and customs of Hui soldiers. There were Imams in the army for slaughtering sheep and cattle to provide Halal meat. On the occasion of the Fast-Breaking Festival, Hui soldiers were allowed to go to the garrison mosque to take part in the holiday activities. Thus it won the confidence and support of the Huis, and its force expanded to over 2000 people. In a period of 5 years from its formation to the end of the war, the Hui Detachment had fought in more than 100 massive battles, capturing over 20 fortified points, wiping out 1300 people of the Japanese puppet army, seizing 20 artilleries, 10 scatter-guns, 1500 rifles and pistols and innumerable military supplies.

Other Hui anti-Japanese forces under the leadership of the Chinese Communist Party appeared during the war of resistance against Japan were: National Anti-Japan Liberation Vanguard founded in Zaozhuang in 1937; the Hui Anti-Japan Army for Saving the Country founded in Cangzhou in the winter of 1937 and led by Liu Zifang (Hui); the Hui Guerrillas founded in Zaozhuang in 1938; the Muslim Battalion founded in Erlong Village, Dingbian County, Anhui Province, in September of 1938;

the Hui Guerrillas founded in Liuhezhu Town, Jiangsu Province, in the end of 1939; the Hui Brigade of Military Subarea of the Hebei and Shandong Border founded in 1939; the Hui Anti-Japanese Guerrillas founded in Luoning County in July of 1944, and led by Ding Zhenxing (Hui, also called Ding Laoliu).

On the other hand, some reactionary forces both at home and abroad took advantage of Islam to disintegrate the Muslim military force to realize their political ambition. The Japanese invaders did this most often. Having captured North China, the Japanese plotted and set up the puppet "China Islamic Federation" to control the Huis with their traitors. They created many problems among the peoples of Inner Mongolia and Xinjiang so that they could reap unfair gains. Tsarist Russia attempted vainly to found an independent Islamic country in Xinjiang to destabilize the Northwest frontier of China. Due to the unity of all nationalities in China and the vigilance and determination of Muslims in these regions, the intrigue of the imperialists failed to succeed.

5. Striving against Insults and Discrimination

The Qing Dynasty was overthrown in the Revolution of 1911, but the successive regimes of both the Northern Warlords and the Republic practiced a policy of ethnic bias and political oppression towards Muslims. They did not acknowledge the rights of the Huis as an ethnic group deserved. These political factors led to insults and discrimination towards the Huis either orally or in publications, with the purpose of manufacturing ethnic conflicts. In this situation, Muslims all rose up to clarify any problems when they could not stand it any more. Cases of insults against Islam and the Muslims' efforts against these insults emerged endlessly.

In July of 1931, a paper entitled "The Story Why the Muslims in Southeast Asian Don't Eat Pork" by Wei Juezhong was published in the 4th issue of the 2nd volume of "New Asia" magazine, whose chief editor was Dai Jitao, a founding member of the Kuomintang, to undisguisedly insult Islam. It deeply hurt the Muslims both at home and abroad, and aroused the indignation of Huis throughout the country. They wrote to the editorial office of "Yue Hua", a Hui cultural publication, to request it to lodge a protest and make representation to it on their behalf. The principal of "Yue Hua" wrote to Dai Jitao at once to lodge a solemn protest, severely criticizing its faults and requesting it to apologize and clear it up in due form, and guarantee that they would never publish papers of this kind any more. "New Asia" magazine replied and admitted that the paper was sheer nonsense, and it was a great shame for them. In the 6th issue of the 2nd volume of "New Asia" they cleared it up.

In September of 1932, "Why Muslims Don't Eat Pork" written by Lou Zikuang, a paper that stopped at nothing to defile Islam and Muslims, was published in the 14th issue of the 1st volume of "Nanhua Literature", run by Zeng Zhongming, vice minister for Railways of the Nanjing Kuomintang government. The Huis in Shanghai filled with indignation recommended Ha Shaofu and two others to make representation to it on their behalf, requesting the office of "Nanhua Literature" to apologize and publish refuting papers of the Huis. When the news arrived in Beijing, Muslims of all circles came to a conclusion that successive cases of insult towards Islam were by no means only directed at Hui Muslims in one place or at one time, and they should unite all Huis in the entire country to make representation to the government. Soon after that they organized Islam Protection Group of the Huis in Northern China and dispatched representatives to Nanjing to present a petition, putting forwards the following requests to the Nanjing Kuomintang Government: 1. to dismiss the chief editor of "Nanhua Literature" Zeng Zhongming; 2. to order "Nanhua Literature" to stop publishing; 3. to punish Lou Zikuang, author of the paper. However, what one never expected was that "Little Pig" written by Lin Lan which contained insulting comments against Islam was published by Beixin Publishing House Shanghai just around the time when the former case had not yet been settled. Hearing this, Huis in Shanghai were

© Fenghuang Mosque in Hangzhou.

infuriated, and they chose Da Pusheng and others to represent them and present a petition to Nanjing. As the "Nanhua Literature" incident had not yet been settled, the representatives of Islam Protection Group of the Huis in Northern China were still in Nanjing when they arrived. So the two delegations allied with each other and explained in detail the facts of the incidents of "Nanhua Literature" and the Beixin Publishing House to the Government, requesting a fair and just settlement. On November 8, the Nanjing Kuomintang Government declared ethnic equality and religious freedom and put an end to the incidents by ordering "Nanhua Literature" to stop publishing, punishing the writer, sealing up the Beixin Publishing House and punishing the ones who were responsible for.

In early 1936, another incident of insulting and discriminating Muslims took place in Beijing. On March 30, "The Citizen" newspaper published "Bizarre Customs", a paper that insulted Muslim women, and was reprinted by "Time Speech" newspaper soon after. It rekindled the indignation of Muslims in Beijing. Only when the two newspapers made corrections and apologized openly was the problem finally settled. "The World Daily" and "The Citizen" reprinted this paper under the title of "Hami Produces Beauty" on April 5 and 6 respectively, so it was considered to be deliberately in defiance. It aroused the public anger of Muslims. A number of Muslims fought with the staff of the two newspaper offices£¨ resulting in bloodshed. Armed police intervened afterwards and the incident calmed down. As the impact of the incident continued to spread, the Kuomintang Government had to mediate and settle the problem. The two newspaper offices were compelled to apologize in its important new columns in big lettering for three days, and throw daylight on the whole event in "The World Daily" and "The Morning Paper". Firmly requested by Muslims, Beijing authorities also guaranteed that: 1). the municipal government would strictly prohibit insults on the Huis in accordance with the laws that had already been in practice; 2). the Beijing Journalist Association should restrict and supervise its members and would never publish papers insulting Islam, and apologize to all the mosques.

In 1947, there occurred the "Case of September 16th". "Beijing New Paper" published an anonymous paper in entitle of "Pig" to humiliate Islam. It deeply hurt Muslims and triggered great indignation of Hui Muslims. They held the "Convention on Defending Islam concerning the 'Beijing New Paper Incident'". On the next day, thousands of Hui Muslims wearing white caps marched on demonstration to the office of "Beijing New Paper"

from Niujie. Ignoring the strong protest of the Muslims, some newspapers in Beijing published a paper simultaneously in the name of the Press Association to support "Beijing New Paper". The Central News Agency of the Kuomintang government also shielded it with the excuse of misunderstanding of Islamic doctrines, and it aroused even more anger from Hui Muslims. They presented a petition to the government, and by then the Beijing authorities had to acknowledge their faults. "Beijing New Paper" also made a self-criticism in the newspaper and its principal went to the Beijing Muslim Association to apologize. The municipal government reiterated its command to respect religions and prohibit insults on them. The mayor addressed Hui Muslims to show his utmost solace and put an end to the incident.

Moreover, similar incidents also occurred in other places. In November 1933, the Guangyi Publishing House in Nanchang was commissioned to sell "The Romance of Fragrant Imperial Concubine" published by Jingzhi Publishing House in Shanghai, which contained words insulting Islam and the Prophet Muhammad. "The Interesting Hearsay of Three Kids" published in the 17th issue of "Beijing Secondary School Newsletter" in 1933 contained content humiliating Islam. In December of the same year, "Industry and Commercial Daily" in Tangshan published a paper cooking up a story that Huis practiced a custom of polyandry. On May 23, 1934, "The Oriental Express" in Beijing published a paper titled "On the Throne" by Zhi Xuan, which contained words disgracing the Prophet Muhammad. On June 18 of the same year, Dacheng, Zhili and Weiwen three publishing houses put on sale "Nian Gengyao's Conquering March to the West", in which there were several comments insulting Muslims. This incident resulted in violent conflicts. Still there were other incidents of this sort: dramas that insulted Huis were played in Shanghai and Hebei, and textbooks used in these places contained content that insulted Islam; someone with evil purpose even threw pork into Muslim food shops in certain places. All these incidents mentioned above indicates that there existed ethnic inequality during the Republic Period.

6. Situation of Islam in Xinjiang during the Republic Period

From 1911 when the Revolution of 1911 broke out to 1949 when New China was founded, Xinjiang successively went through four regimes of Yang Zengxin, Jin Shuren, Sheng Shicai and direct dominance from the Kuomintang government.

Yang Zengxin, a successful candidate in the highest imperial examination in the Qing Dynasty, was born in Mengzi County, Yunnan Province, where Muslims lived in compact community. He was appointed as the governor of Xinjiang after the Revolution of 1911, and changed to the post of provincial chairman afterwards. Having spent his official career mostly in Hezhou and Xinjiang where Muslims had an overwhelming majority, Yang Zengxin knew a lot about the doctrine and sects of Islam. So he adopted dual tactics of both mollification and suppression towards the Muslims in Xinjiang, not oppressing them excessively lest the major ethnic groups in this region rose to oppose him. He made use of Islam to comfort the Muslim mass

144

© Dingzhou Mosque in Hebei, constructed in the Yuan Dynasty.

and took advantage of the ethnic conflicts to disintegrate them so that they were no able to unite together under the standard of Islam.

Yang Zengxin was active in striving for the support of the upper circles of the Muslims in Xinjiang, giving preferential treatment to the nobilities of the Uighurs so as to use them to comfort and control the Muslims. Not only did he fully acknowledge the titles and ranks of the nobilities of the minority groups in Xinjiang that were conferred by the Qing Dynasty and reserved all their privileges, but also reported to the Government of the Northern Warlords for reconfirmation and promotion so as to solidify his ruling. Yang Zengxin also took advantage of the conflicts among the ethnic groups and clans to make them contain each other to maintain the peace of his separatist regime.

By the end of the Qing Dynasty, the land army and patrol battalion in Xinjiang were dominated by Hans. In order to keep Huis and other Muslim peoples under control and pin down the former army dominated by Hans, Yang Zengxin organized the Hui Army, with which he could also pin down the armed escort dominated by the Uighurs and the cavalry of the Kazaks. Thus, not only the people who constituted the majority in Xinjiang were kept under control, but the Hans were also pinned down. To maintain the social stability of Xinjiang and solidify his regime, Yang Zengxin adopted a serial of measures to restrain the "Double-Pan" thoughts (Pan-Islamism and Pan-Turkism appeared in the end of the 19th century and the beginning of the 20th century). He took strict precautions towards foreigners to Xinjiang by having their identity clarified, not allowing them to engage with locals, or expelling them and burning the propaganda material they distributed. He also prohibited foreigners from running schools or be teachers in Xinjiang. As for Chinese who colluded with foreigners to propagandize the "Double-Pan" thoughts, he resorted to severe punishment. The foreign teachers who openly spread the "Double-Pan" thoughts in new schools would be expelled by the local government, and the school they served would be closed down as well.

Jin Shuren, a student of Yang Zengxin, came to Xinjiang after he graduated from the High School of Gansu and was appointed county magistrate of Aksu and other counties, and was promoted to the position of director of the Provincial Civil Affairs Department of Xinjiang in 1926. He was appointed chairman of Xinjiang by the Republic Government after Yang Zengxin was assassinated. Jin Shuren held an attitude of strict precaution towards religious matters. His policy of ethnic and religious discrimination and suppression intensified the contradictions among the ethnic groups in Xinjiang. He arranged refugees unwisely at the cost of Uighur farmers' field and their irrigation systems. His estrepement damaged pasture lands and impacted the subsistence of the Kazaks, Khalkhas and other peoples who lived on it. Taking advantage of the opportunity to enlarge the army, he squeezed out most of the Hui military officials and replaced them with the Hans from Gansu. Many of his officials and soldiers held an attitude of Han chauvinism towards Muslim groups. It aroused the great indignation of the Muslims of all nationalities and resulted in violent conflicts. The Accident of Xiaobao in 1931 triggered an insurrection and led to the collapse of Jin Shuren's regime.

◎ Eidkah Mosque in Kashgar, Xinjiang.

On February 27, 1931, Zhang Guohu, a platoon leader of the Han garrison in Xiaobao, a small town at the east of Hami, took a local Uighur woman by force, ignoring the ethnic tradition of the Uighurs. The local Uighur peasants marched to Qincheng Town and rose in revolt that night. The local garrison was wiped out, and it soon developed into a province-wide uprising. The regime of Jin Shuren finally collapsed, and Sheng Shicai took over and became the new warlord ruling Xinjiang.

Sheng Shicai was born to a military family in Shenyang. He had been to Japan twice for learning, and held a post in the general headquarters of the revolutionary army of the Republic after he turned to China. In 1930, he came to Xinjiang. Taking advantage of the uprising in Hami, Sheng Shicai built up his feudal warlord regime. He had always flaunted ethnic equality and religious freedom, but when the political situation changed, he came to bloodily persecute personages within minority groups and adopted a policy of eliminating Islam. On April 12, 1934, Xinjiang Provincial Government issued its Administration Declaration (generally called "Eight Declarations") which placed religious problem above all the others. Soon afterwards, it formulated "Six Policies" (namely 1. opposing imperialism; 2. favoring the Soviet Union; 3. insisting on ethnic equality; 4. being honest and upright; 5. maintaining peace; 6. being constructive) as its complete guiding line. In the initial period to carry out these policies, it produced some positive effects. For example, the authorities admitted personages from ethnic minority groups into government, and ethnic contradictions were mitigated to some extent as a result. At the Second Provincial Populace Representative Assembly of Xinjiang, the Xinjiang Populace Federation was set up to deal specially with ethnic relations. It is also at this conference that the ethnic name for the Uighurs, the Khalkhas, the Tajiks and the Tatars were defined, and a number of mass organizations were established to promote ethnic culture and improve Muslims' education. However, the Six Policies in fact were only a tactic by which Sheng Shicai could build up his autocracy. Once he had held his ground in Xinjiang, Sheng Shicai began to persecute Muslims, accusing them of plotting revolt. He roped in prestigious and powerful people from minority groups at first, and then dragged them into the cases of revolt and sentenced them to imprisonment or even execution.

Xinjiang entered the stage of the direct ruling of Kuomintang after Sheng Shicai left. Motivated by calls for peace at home and abroad and due to its military failures, the Kuomintang Government dispatched Zhang Zhizhong for peace negotiations in Dihua, at which a peace protocol was signed and the Provincial Coalition Government was established, which soon disintegrated. In January 1949, Bao'erhan took up the post of chairman of the Xinjiang Provincial Government. On September 19, he telephoned Mao Zedong, indicating that he had decided to break away from the Kuomintang government. On October 20, the vanguard of the People's Liberation Army entered Dihua and garrisoned there, and Xinjiang was liberated peacefully.

CHAPTER 4
ISLAM IN THE INITIAL PERIOD OF NEW CHINA

In over 1,000 years from the Tang and Song dynasties when Islam was introduced into China up until 1949 when New China was founded, Chinese Muslims had enjoyed many glories, and were subjected to misfortunes as well. In the Qing Dynasty and the period when warlords took over the throne, Muslims (in the Northwest in particular) were subjected to brutal persecutions and killings, and lived in precarious circumstances. After New China was founded in 1949, the people's government practiced a policy of ethnic equality and religious freedom. It gave Chinese Muslims of all nationalities a new life and made them truly enjoy equality in economics, politics and ethnic affairs, and religious freedom. The national census in 2000 shows that there are 10 minority groups with a total population of over 20 million in China that take Islam as their national faith. They are distributed mainly in Xinjiang, Ningxia, Gansu, Qinghai, Yunnan and Henan, while there is also a considerable Muslim population in Shaanxi, Hebei and Shandong. Nowadays, under the leadership of the Chinese Communist Party, Muslims of all ethnicities in China work hard in all walks of life, striving for ethnic unity, social stability and prosperity.

1. Being Active in the Construction of New China

After New China was founded in 1949, Chinese Muslims of all ethnicities acquired equal political rights and religious freedom, which were written into the constitution. The people's governments in all areas attached great importance to protecting religious sites such as mosques and mausoleums and respecting Muslims' faith and their habits and customs when they undertook to stabilize the social order and restore the economy. For example, the stipulation issued by the State Council concerning the minority groups' holidays and festivals prescribes that Muslims of all ethnicities enjoy days off on the occasions of 'Id al-Fitr (Festival of Fast-Breaking) and 'Id al-Kurban (Festival of Sacrifice). The State Council also issued an order that the sheep and cattle used by Muslims of all ethnicities for their three major festivals are exempt from slaughtering tax. The Ministry of Finance sent out a notice that all land used to build mosques and mausoleums are exempt from land tax. The State Council instructed local governments that if names given to certain minority groups in history, or names of certain places and steles and inscribed boards concerning minority groups contained an indication of discrimination or insult towards

© Xielijie Mosque in Hong Kong.

minority groups, they should cease using them, or be corrected or sealed up. In places where Muslims lived in compact communities, the system of regional autonomy of ethnic minorities is practiced and people's governments at all levels were set up, like the Xinjiang Uighur Autonomous Region (established on October 1, 1955), the Changji Hui Autonomous Prefecture in Xinjiang (established on November 27, 1954), the Ningxia Hui Autonomous Region (established on October 25,

1958), the Zhangjiachuan Hui Autonomous County in Gansu (established on July 1, 1953), the Menyuan Hui Autonomous County in Qinghai (established on December 19, 1953), the Hualong Hui Autonomous County (established on March 2, 1954), and Dachang Hui Autonomou Region in Hebei (established on December 7, 1955). Thus, Muslims of all ethnicities became the masters of their own life, and started to manage all their own affairs.

As their fortunes radically changed, Chinese Muslims started a new life. They devoted themselves with full enthusiasm into the great cause of the socialist construction and reformation of New China, and contributed their bit to restoring the state economy and accomplishing the First 5-Year Plan.

1). ACTIVELY SUPPORTING THE WAR TO RESIST U.S. AGGRESSION AND AID KOREA

In 1950, a nationwide campaign to "Resist U.S. Aggression and Aid Korea, Protect Home and Defend Country" was launched in China. Responding to the call of the state, Muslims of all ethnicities did their best to increase production and practice austerity. They were very active in patriotic activities such as saluting the voluntary army and contributing planes and artillery.

2). Carrying out Land Reform in Line with Local Condition

Muslims in the countryside were not satisfied only with their rebirth in political life. Inspired by land reform in Han areas, they also wanted to carry out land reform, to realize real self-liberation and develop the countryside economy. Responding to the request of Muslims, the people's government systematically launched land reform in line with the local situation in places where Muslims were comparatively concentrated. After the land reforms were accomplished, Muslims of all ethnicities came to take part in the cause of the socialist reconstruction and made great efforts to strengthen ethnic unity and develop the minority groups' economy, and accomplished tasks to restore the state economy as a result.

2. The Formation of Islamic Organizations and Their Activities in China

In 1952, well-known Chinese Muslims including Bao'erhan Shaxidi, Liu Geping, Saifuding Aizezi, Da Pusheng and Ma Jian, proposed to organize the China Islamic Association and were greeted with an immediate response by Islamic circles and Muslims throughout the country. On July 27, 1952, 53

© The inaugural meeting of the China Islamic Association in 1953.

157

representatives elected from various ethnicities held the preparatory meeting and formed the preparatory committee for forming the China Islamic Association. Bao'erhan Shaxidi was elected as director, Da Pusheng as deputy-director, and 27 others as members of the committee.

On May 11, 1953, the First National Representative Assembly of the China Islamic Association was held in Beijing with 111 representatives attending, symbolizing the formal establishment of the China Islamic Association. The Assembly formulated and passed the constitution of the Association, which indicated that the purpose of the Association was to: assist the people's government to carry out the policy of religious freedom; develop the fine traditions of Islam; represent the legal rights and interests of the Islamic population; unite Muslims of all ethnicities to be both patriotic to the country and faithful to Islam; develop and strengthen friendly contacts and exchanges with Muslims all over the world; and maintain the world peace. Bao'erhan Shaxidi was elected as director of the Association and 83 others as members. It was stipulated in the constitution that the supreme body of the Association was the National Congress of Chinese Islam. It was an unprecedented united Islamic organization in the history of China, which built a bridge between the government and Muslims. Soon afterwards, local Islamic associations were set up successively in provinces, autonomous regions and those municipalities directly under the central government where Muslim lived in compact communities, among which the Xinjiang Autonomous Regions Islamic Association was founded earliest in 1956. These Islamic associations at all levels have been playing an important role in assisting the government to carry out the policy of religious freedom, contacting Islamic persons of note and departments in charge of ethnic and religious affairs, and managing internal Islamic affairs.

In consideration of letting the world know the actual situation of Muslims in New China and promoting friendly contacts with foreign Muslims, as early as just before the Association was founded, the preparatory committee of the Association had organized the first pilgrim delegation soon after the founding of New China to resume Chinese Muslims' pilgrimage. The delegation comprised 16 members from the whole country with Imam Da Pusheng (Hui) and Yiming Mahesum (Uighur) as president and vice-president respectively. In early August 1952, the delegation arrived in Pakistan via Hong Kong and India. Due to sanctions that the western powers had applied against China and the rumor that New China was wiping

◎ Premier Zhou Enlai met with a foreign Muslim delegation; the leaders of the China Islamic Association Bao'erhan Shaxidi, Zhang Jie and Liu Pinyi were present.

out religions and persecuting Muslims, in addition to the fact that diplomatic relations with Saudi Arabia had not yet been established, the delegation came to a premature end.

In April of 1955, Imam Da Pusheng, vice-president of the China Islamic Association, attended the Bandung Conference held in Bandung, Indonesia, as religious advisor to Premier Zhou Enlai. The Bandung Conference was a great success in Chinese diplomatic history and gave a precious opportunity to Chinese Muslims to allow their dreams of performing pilgrimage come true. Imam Da Pusheng as well as other Chinese attendants introduced to the representatives from Islamic countries the policy of religious freedom that the Chinese government had been practicing and the progress and development that Chinese Muslims had accomplished in New China. With common efforts from Premier Zhou Enlai and Egyptian president Nasir and Saudi King Faisal, the first pilgrimage delegation of the New China with Imam Da Pusheng as president and 19 others as members arrived in Mecca to perform pilgrimage in August 1955. The whole world, Islamic countries in particular, paid attention to this event. In 1956, the second pilgrimage delegation of New China comprising 37 persons led by Bao'erhan arrived in Mecca, and Saudi King received it three times. All the members of the delegation kissed the Black Stone, and Bao'erhan was even invited to attend the ceremony of washing Ka'bah and accepted a piece of Ka'bah curtain and an Arab costume as gifts from the

© The location of the China Islamic Association in the 1950's---Dongsi Mosque in Beijing.

Saudi King. From 1955 to 1964, the China Islamic Association had organized 10 pilgrim delegations, with 132 persons altogether.

On the occasion of 'Id al-Kurban in July of 1957, the trial issue of "Muslims in China", a comprehensive magazine produced by the China Islamic Association, was published in Beijing. It was this magazine that introduced the main activities of the Association to Muslims throughout the country, and reflected the situation and events of Muslims as well. The magazine acted not only as a bridge between the higher and lower levels, but also a link for the Islamic associations at all levels and Muslims to exchange information, experience and to strengthen their contacts. In 1959, the magazine was suspended, by then 24 issues had been published.

On November 21, 1955, the China Islamic Institute was established in Beijing. The purpose of the Institute was to foster Imams who were both patriotic to the country and faithful to Islam. The students of the Institute were mainly prospective Muslim youths who had learnt a little about Islam in mosques. By graduation, they were to be in possession of considerable Islamic knowledge and high school level Chinese language ability, and could handle religious matters within mosques, be able to read Arabic scriptures and simple oral and written translation. The major courses offered at the Institute were: theology, the Holy Qur'an (including Qur'an recitation and annotation), Hadith, Islamic Law and Arabian literature. Chinese (mainly for Uighur classes), history, geography and politics were also taught as minor courses in the Institute.

In the beginning and middle of the 1950's, great importance was attached to the publication and study of Islamic scriptures. The China Islamic Association photo lithographed the original Arabic edition of the Holy Qur'an three times, and a number of selected editions. In 1950, the Publishing House of Beijing University published "The Holy Qur'an" (first half) translated by Ma Jian. It comprises 8 volumes and 6 chapters, and annotations and "A Brief Introduction to the Holy Qur'an" by the translator. With great efforts of the China Islamic Association, many publishing houses and Arabic experts, a number of picture books were published during this period of time, including "Chinese Muslims' Life", "Muslims in China" and "Chinese Muslims' Religious Life", with captions in Chinese, Arabic, English, French, and Malay. The constitution of the People's Republic of China was also translated into Arabic and distributed home and abroad. A picture book "Beijing Muslims' Life" with trilingual caption in Chinese, Arabic and English, and a book "The Holy Qur'an and Women's Rights and Status" compiled in line with the Marriage Law of the New China were published. And the following works that were published in this period of time were of special importance: "The History of Islamic Law" translated by Pang Shiqian filled the gap in the field of studies on Islamic Law in China. "An Illustration to Islamic Scriptures" translated by Ma Jian became one of the basic textbooks of domestic Islamic education. "Islam and Society" translated by Chen Keli expounds the relationship between Islam and social development. Speed-up textbook "Islamic Book" compiled by Zhang Hongtao gives an introduction to common knowledge on Islam and attached 19 pictures to demonstrate how to perform prayers. In addition, "Life of the Prophet Muhammad" translated and edited by Ma Chongyi, "Hadith" (first volume) translated by Chen Keli, "Muhammad's Sword", a collection of essays by Ma Jian concerning the history and culture of Islam, "Arabian Poems" translated by Ma Anli and Ma Xuehai, were all of great importance to help people rightly understand Islam and promote mutual understanding and unity with Non-Muslims.

In the autumn of 1958, impacted by "Leftist" thoughts, the works on studying Islamic doctrine and the history of and culture of Chinese Muslims, and publishing Islamic books and scriptures was suspended until 18 years later when the Cultural Revolution came to an end in 1976.

· · · · · · · · · · · · · · · · · · ·

3. Democratic Reform to Religious Systems of Chinese Islam

Chinese Muslims started a new political life after the land reforms and socialist reconstruction was accomplished. However, the feudal privileges and system of exploitation were still in existence in religious fields, greatly hampering the development of social production and the improvement of Muslims' life. In the Northwest in particular, there still existed the religious domination of Menhuans (special Islamic sects in China) and a heavy religious burden, so it became necessary to carry out certain reform to religious systems of Chinese Islam.

From 1958 to 1960, under the leadership of the central authorities, a couple of democratic reforms were carried out concerning certain aspects of religious systems of Chinese Islam. In line with the actual situation and basic principles for reform, the religious systems of Chinese Islam was classified into three categories: those severely hampering the development of production were of the first, 11 items altogether, these must be reformed; those not being much of an obstacle were of the second, 5 items altogether, these could remained unformed; those being no obstacle at all were of the third, these definitely could remain unformed, and proper solutions would be worked out for their existence.

The feudal privileges and the system of exploitation that existed in the religious system of Chinese Islam in the Northwest was basically abolished after the democratic reform was successfully carried out. Muslims were liberated from religious feudal oppression and exploitation, and production developed a great deal as a result.

The democratic reform to the religious system of Chinese Islam conformed to the trend of the times and exerted a great influence on the social progress and development of politics, economy and culture of the Muslim ethnic regions. However, affected by "Leftist" thoughts, some blunders were produced as well; some Muslims legal religious activities were interfered or restrained.

CHAPTER 5
CHINESE ISLAM IN NEW TIMES

After the policy of opening up to the outside world was put into practice in 1978, China entered a new era, and the Chinese Islamic cause was resumed and developed comprehensively as well.

1.Implementing Policy on Religion and Restoring Religious Organizations

After the Third Plenary Session of the 11th Party Central Committee was held, the Central Committee of the Communist Party, the State Council, and the Party committees and governments at all levels began to bring order out of the chaos which resulted from the Cultural Revolution (1966-1976), and

© Hui Muslims at salat al-'Idain (festival prayer).

169

the wrong charges and persecution of Islamic persons of note and common Muslims in all previous political movements were redressed and their reputation rehabilitated.

Restoring and opening religious sites was a very important link in carrying out the policy of religious freedom. When mosques and simple religious sites were opened in succession, the government allocated certain sums of special funds to facilitate maintaining some well-known ancient mosques and other Islamic relics and historic sites. Among the mosques that had been opened 64 were in Beijing, 53 were in Tianjin (including a Hui service center), 6 were in Shanghai. By the end of the 1980's, there were 2,800 mosques, 80 mausoleums, 5 Khanqas (shrine of Menhuan) and 2,900 Imams in Gansu; 118 mosques in Shaanxi; 2,700 mosques and 3,600 Imams in Ningxia; 867 Mosques and 3,562 Imams in Qinghai; and over 20,000 mosques and spots in Xinjiang. According to statistics of nationwide religious sites registration conducted from 1994 to 1996, there were altogether 34,014 registered mosques in the entire country by 1996, among which 23,331 were in Xinjiang; 2,610 were in Gansu; 2,984 were in Ningxia; 817 were in Henan, 728 were in Yunnan; 397 were in Hebei and 409 were in Shandong. At present, the total number of mosques in the entire country is equal to this.

◎ China Islamic Association holds national Holy Qur'an recitation competition every two years, by then all outstanding Qaris (reciters) gather in Beijing.

The China Islamic Association resumed activities. In April of 1980, the 4th National Representative Assembly of the China Islamic Association was held in Beijing, 256 representatives of 10 Muslim minority groups from all over the country attended. It was a conference that was held 17 years after 1963, symbolizing the fact that the China Islamic Association had resumed its activities. Islamic organizations at provincial, regional and municipal levels were restored or reestablished successively. By the end of 1995, 25 provinces, autonomous regions and municipalities directly under the central government had set up Islamic associations. The number of Islamic associations at city

© In January 2000, the 7th National Representative Assembly of the China Islamic Association was held in Beijing.

and county levels reached 420, and the number of Imams and Mullahs reached 45,000.

The China Islamic Association has held 7 representative assemblies up to now. The 7th Representative assembly was held on January 27-30 2000, with 324 representatives attending. It was a milestone of the development of the Chinese Islamic cause. The Assembly heard the work report by Wan Yaobin, vice president of the China Islamic Association, entitled "To unite together and make progress, carry forward the cause and forge ahead into the future" and subtitled "Strive for the Chinese Islamic cause in the new century". He reviewed the successes and failures that Chinese Islam had experienced in the last century, especially the last 20 years, pointing out that in the past 6 years, the China Islamic Association had efficiently and creatively done many things focusing on domestic Islamic work, and made useful exploration in certain respects as to how to guide Islam to adapt itself to socialist society. The mosques' democratic administration standard and the consciousness of legal religious activities had been promoted a great deal. And the "Two Competitions and One Appraisal" (namely the Holy Qur'an recitation competition and preaching competition, and model mosque appraisal) in particular had effectively motivated the work of the Islamic associations in all places. The report also set the objectives and the directions for the development of Chinese Islam in the new century, pointing out that in the circumstances of the new era, the China

© China Islamic Association holds al-Wa'z (preaching) Competition every two year.

Islamic Association would further clear up its own position and situation, give full play to its own advantages, actively participate in the great cause of the development of western regions, motivate Islam to adapt itself to socialist society, strengthen ethnic unity, vigorously call for united efforts on Islamic work, strongly oppose ethic separatism and religious extremism, maintain social stability and do its bit for the reunification of the motherland.

2. Setting up Regulations and System to Strengthen Mosque Democratic Administration

Nowadays, there are altogether over 35,000 mosques throughout the country, being distributed in all places where Muslims live, and on average there is one mosque for every 600 people. A democratic administrative committee was set up in each mosque after they were reopened. The committee members were elected by all parties concerned consultatively, and were entrusted responsibilities to: arrange religious activities, invite Imam to the mosque, manage donations and rent, maintain and protect the mosque, organize religious staff to study scriptures and doctrine, and coordinate relations with other mosques locally. Furthermore, a number of laws or regulations have been put into practice to promote the democratic administration of mosques, for example the state constituted "Regulations on Administration of Religious Sites" and "Regulations Concerning Foreigners'

◎ In November of 2002, the China Islamic Association cooperated with the Embassy of Iran and jointly held the "Sino-Iran Exhibition on Qur'anic Culture and Art", president of the Association, Imam Chen Guangyuan and the Iranian Ambassador were present.

Religious Activities within the Boundary of the People's Republic of China"; the China Islamic Association formulated "Trial Measures for Mosques' Democratic Administration"; the Xinjiang Islamic Association laid down "Regulations on Mosques' Democratic Administration" and "Patriotic Convention of Islamic Persons of Note"; the Zhangjiachuan County Islamic Association of Gansu also drew up a 10-item "Patriotic Convention"; the Beijing Islamic Association passed the "Constitution of the Mosques' Democratic Administrative Committee of Beijing Municipality", mosques in Shanghai and other places also laid down similar regulations.

Some mosques and Imams afforded to sponsor schools, or even run nurseries, kindergartens, ethnic primary schools and girls' schools, mobilizing both Muslim boys and girls to attend school to attain knowledge and become useful people for the economic construction of ethnic regions, for example, the Urumchi Islamic Association has always been concerned about the special educational needs of handicapped children; the Islamic Association of Linxia Hui Autonomous Prefecture of Gansu Province mobilized all quarters concerned to make donations for education which reached 7 million yuan and ranked first in the province, among which Ma Liang, a Hui peasant entrepreneur in Guanghe County, donated 300,000 yuan to build a primary school; Muchang Mosque in Linxia City raised 300,000 yuan to build a Muslim kindergarten.

Chapter 5 Chinese Islam in New Times

3. Developing Islamic Education and Studies

In June 1982, the China Islamic Institute resumed recruiting students, and opened advanced, undergraduate and short term courses. Up till now it has educated 512 students from 8 ethnic groups including the Huis, the Uighurs, the Kazakhs, the Khalkhas,. Since 1983, 8 Islamic institutes have been set up successively in Shenyang, Lanzhou, Yinchuan, Beijing, Xining, Urumchi and Kunming. Furthermore, various advanced classes for training Imams were opened and Arabic schools were established in some provinces, autonomous regions and municipalities directly under the central government, such as the Kashgar Arabic School, Kezhou Arabic School and Huocheng County Arabic School in Xinjiang.

On September 25, 1981, "Muslims in China" magazine resumed publication; and in 1983, its Uighur language edition started publication, which is a bimonthly with a subscription of several hundred thousand. Acting as the mouthpiece of both the China Islamic Association and of Chinese Muslims, the magazine

plays a unique and irreplaceable role in serving Muslims throughout the country and voicing their wishes. "Studies on the Huis" is a comprehensive academic publication on the Huis' history, culture and social development, and started publication in the early 1990's. In 1980, the full translation of the Holy Qur'an by Ma Jian was published by the Chinese Social Science Press. In 1986, making use of this version, King Fahd Holy Qur'an Printing Complex printed an Arabic-Chinese bilingual Holy Qur'an and presented it to various countries, making it the most popular version in China. In 1988, "Rhymed Translation of the

Holy Qur'an" by Lin Song was published by the publishing house of the Central University for Nationalities. In 1989, "Chinese-Arabic Bilingual Detailed Translation and Annotation of the Holy Qur'an" by Shams Tong Daozhang, an American Chinese, was published by Yilin Publishing House in Nanjing, and in 1999 its revised edition was published. Furthermore, Hui scholars have translated and published some other Islamic scriptures and academic works, among which what is worth mentioning is: Maimaiti Sailai translated the Holy Qur'an into the Uighur language and Abdul Aziz and Mohmaud translated the Holy Qur'an into the Kazakh language, these were published by Ethnic Press in 1987 and 1989 respectively.

To motivate academic research on Islam, a symposium presided in turn by 5 provinces and autonomous regions in the Northwest was held nearly every year with its first in Urumchi in November of 1980, and in Lanzhou of Gansu Province (1981), Xining of Qinghai Province (1982), Xi'an of Shaanxi Province (1983) and YinChuan of Ningxia Hui Autonomous Region (1986) successively. Each time the symposium would focus on a certain theme, and afterwards publish a collection of the thesis. The symposium that had been held 5 times, produced altogether 403 papers and monographs, which played a positive role in motivating academic research on Islam in China and exploring and sorting out documents and data. This regional symposium has been in practice up until now.

The International Seminar on the Huis' History and Culture is another important academic activity that has been held many times. The objective of the seminar is to enhance international exchanges on research on the Huis, develop traditional ethnic culture, promote ethnic unity, inspire ethnic enthusiasm, and pursue the development of economy, progress of society and prosperity of the culture in ethnic regions. Characterized by a strong sense of learning, broad coverage of sphere and rich possession of information, the seminar has attracted much attention from both academic circles and the media at home and abroad. "The 13th Seminar on the Huis' History" held in Nanjing, Jiangsu Province, in September of 2001 is one of the most successful ones. Focusing on the theme of the "Prospect of the Learning on the Huis in the 21st Century", the Seminar suggested ways and means for the development of the Northwest.

The contingent of Chinese Islamic academic workers keeps growing. The institutions of higher learning came to attach importance to fostering a young generation of Islamic academic workers, and some ethnic universities and colleges now offer

© Muslim women everywhere attach great importance to learning.

major courses on Islam. Islamic institutes in all places also offer courses on Islamic doctrine, philosophy, history and culture to foster a new generation of Islamic academic and religious workers. In this period of time, new progress was made on studies of Mosque Education, the Movement of Translating and Writing Scriptures in Chinese, sects and Menhuans, history of Islam, the roles that Islam played for the formation of the Huis and other nationalities, mosque and its social function, Muslims' social movements, religious system, historical documents, steles and inscribed boards concerning Islam in southeast coastal area and so on. Nationwide or provincial Islamic magazines and journals were resumed or started publication one after another, and have published thousands of papers on various aspects of Islam in China. Publishing houses throughout China have published hundreds of books on Islam and minority groups believing in Islam. The offices for sorting out ancient books of minority groups have been set up in some provinces, autonomous regions and municipalities directly under the central government and have published many ancient Islamic works. The China Islamic Association cooperated with several publishing houses and published the "Holy Qur'an" in 1980 with a subscription of over 160,000, "Concise Tafsir", "Pearls of Hadith", a selection of Hadith from both Bukhari and Muslim, "Sharikh al-Wigayi", a scripture on Islamic Law, "Khutbah", "Life of Prophet

◎ Imams from various mosques in Beijing read scriptures or foreign newspapers in the library of Dongsi Mosque.

◎ State councilor Simayi Aimaiti and well-known Muslim historian and linguist Prof. Na Zhong talk to a scholar from Saudi Arabia.

Muhammad", "An Illustration to Islamic Scriptures" translated by Ma Jian and "Nine Years in Egypt" written by Pang Shiqian and so on.

With great efforts from the China Islamic Association, "Chinese Encyclopedia of Islam" was published in 1994, which won the First National Dictionary Prize and the Second State Books Highest Prize in 1995 and 1996 respectively.

In the provinces, autonomous regions and municipalities directly under the central government where Muslims live in compact communities, great importance is attached to studying and publishing Islamic scriptures. The Xinjiang government has presented 90,000 Holy Qur'ans and 100,000 "Sahih al-Bukhari" in the Uighur language to Islamic dignitaries and common Muslims alike. The Jiangsu Provincial Islamic Association has cooperated with the Yilin Publishing House in Nanjing and published the "Holy Qur'an" translated by Tong Daozhang. The Yunnan Provincial Islamic Association printed 2000 Holy Qur'ans from carved printing plates made during the Qing Dynasty, and has sorted out over 100 sets of such plates in the Chinese, Arabic and Persian languages, more than 70 of which are complete and usable. The Division for Studies on the Huis of Ningxia Social Academy has published many Islamic scriptures and works such as "A Guide to Islam", "True Explanation to the Right Religion & Great Learning of Islam & Righter Answers to Truth-Seekers", "Sharikh al-Wigayi", "History of Islam in Arabia", "Fine Collection of Historic Chinese Islamic Newspapers", "Collection of Documents and Data on the Huis and Islam", "Abstract to the Written and Translated Works on Chinese Islam", and "A Faithful Record of Chinese Muslims' Pilgrimage". The Gansu Provincial Islamic Association published "Going around Kabah" written by Yang Guangrong. The Shanghai Municipal Islamic Association undertook "Exhibition of Islamic Relics in

Shanghai". The provincial Islamic associations in eastern China have held seminars in Suzhou, Shanghai, Quanzhou, Hangzhou and Jinan on Islamic literature and the history of the southeast coastal region. In July 1982, the Islamic Study Society was founded in Ningxia, and was followed by other similar mass cultural groups in the Northwest, such as the Islamic Cultural Study Society set up in Xi'an, which has successfully held three seminars on Islamic cultural since 1994, and compiled and published three collections of thesis called "Collected Essays on Islamic Culture".

· ·

4. Participating Actively in the Socialist Construction of "Two Civilizations"

Guided and motivated by the China Islamic Association and local Islamic associations throughout China, Islamic dignitaries and the Muslim masses have been active in the socialist construction for modernization since the 1980's, and made great contributions to the development of the state economy. And in the mean time governments and departments at all levels pay much attention to fostering Muslim professionals. In the last 20 years, the literacy rate of Chinese Muslims has continued to rise. At present, there are 21 colleges and universities with 30,000 students in Xinjiang, and 7 colleges with nearly 10,000 students in Ningxia, of which Muslim students account for a considerable percentage. There are a great number of Muslims working in various fields such as high technology, industry, agriculture, education and medicine.

Muslims in Beijing have advantage in developing the third industry - individual commerce and township enterprises.

Muslims in the Northwest have achieved considerable development in food and other growing industries such as clothing, embroidery, food processing, flock and herd breeding, transportation, electrical equipment, tourism and real estate, and certain products of theirs have entered the international market. They also take advantage of their friendly contacts with Arab Islamic countries to develop foreign trade, open markets in Western and Central Asia, and attract foreigners to travel and invest in China to improve the development of the economy and culture in ethnic regions.

As the state economy and Muslims' living standard continue to develop, Islamic dignitaries and the Muslims masses have shown unprecedented enthusiasm towards the construction of a socialist spiritual civilization.

Since the reform and the policy of opening up to the outside world were put into practice in 1987, there have been a considerable number of Muslims representatives from minority groups working in government, the people's congress and the political consultative conference at all levels, discussing state matters, participating in the administering and supervising of state affairs along with representatives elected by the people of all ethnicities throughout the country. Vice chairman of the National

◎ In March of 1987, Simayi Aimaiti was with the Uighur representatives of the 5th National Representative Assembly of the China Islamic Association in Beijing.

People's Congress of China Tiemu'er Dawumaiti, state councilor Simayi Aimaiti, vice chair of the Chinese People's Political Consultative Conference Bai Lichen all are Muslim. Statistics shows that there are 101 Muslims among the representatives of the National People's Congress and 64 among the members of the Chinese People's Political Consultative Conference.

Due to correct and comprehensive implementation of the policies on religion and ethnic affairs and education aimed at promoting patriotism and against ethnic separatism and religious extremism, unity among the ethnic groups and Islamic sects has improved a great deal. Many mosques and Imams were chosen as "Model Mosque" or "Model Imam". The China Islamic Association chose through public appraisal 100 mosques as "Model Mosques", it has motivated Islamic circles throughout the country to make more of a contribution to the construction of the two socialist civilizations.

Sponsoring education is a fine tradition of Islam. Everywhere in the country, Islamic organizations and Imams (Mullahs) have always been active in contributing money to primary and secondary schools and running nurseries, kindergartens, ethnic primary schools and girls' schools, motivating Muslim youths to attend school and become useful people for the construction of ethnic regions.

To spread the Islamic spirit of "ordering people to do good and stopping people from doing evil" is another fine tradition of

© Muslim entrepreneur contributes money to sponsor Muslim youths' schooling.

Islam, and also an important act to guide Islam to adapt itself to socialist society. Particularly in recent years, people of insight in Chinese Islamic circles have tried to

◎ In July of 2001, China Islamic Association took part in the International Islamic Cultural Expo in Brunei, president of the Association Imam Chen Guangyuan introduced Chinese Muslims' general situation to Sultan Bolkia.

make explanations concerning Islamic doctrine and scriptures that are in line with the times. They have begun with writing and preaching new al-Wa'z (sermons) and have achieved delightful effects.

What is worth mention is that the China Islamic Guidance Committee was established on April 23, 2001. It is composed of 16 patriotic and faithful Imams and Mullahs, who are of noble character, with high prestige and in possession of rich Islamic knowledge. Imam Chen Guangyuan was elected as its chairman. The purpose of the Committee is to offer explanations on religious and social problems facing Muslims in contemporary times,

◎ A group of Hajjis from Xinjiang have a photo taken as memento in front of the Chinese national flag at the Chinese Hajjis' camp at Minah.

opposing religious extremism, maintaining the purity of the Islamic faith, and motivating Islam to adapt itself to socialist society. After a year's hard work of investigation, research, writing, revision, trial preaching and seeking opinions, the "Collection of New al-Wa'z" (first volume) was published in Chinese and Uighur languages as a model for Islamic sermon by the Religious Culture Press in early August of 2001. The Committee presented 120,000 copies of this book (both Chinese and Uighur language versions) to Islamic circles in Xinjiang to regulate the contents of sermons in mosques there. At the same time, it motivated key provinces such as Xinjiang, Gansu, Ningxia, Inner Mongolia and Yunnan to carry out the large-scale work of training Islamic workers. At present, the second volume of "Collection of New al-Wa'z" is being compiled. The commitment of the China Islamic Guidance Committee has become a positive force in promoting social progress, making Islam accepted and understood better in the broader socialist society, and laying a solid foundation both theoretically and practically for the further nationalization of Islam.

To run Islamic colleges and schools of various kinds well and foster qualified Islamic workers is also a great job which

◎ Vice-president and secretary-general of the China Islamic Association Yu Zhengui went to Ningxia to seek advice for the preparation of teaching material for Islamic institutes.

© China Islamic Institute.

determines the future of Chinese Islam. Starting with compiling
teaching material, the China Islamic Association positively seeks
reform to the teaching methods in Islamic institutes. In late May
2001, it held a conference in Beijing to coordinate compiling the
unified teaching material for Islamic institutes in all places and
all levels. It is the first specialized meeting held by a nationwide
religious organization for comprehensive study on compiling
religious teaching material, and also a milestone-like fundamental
construction program in the history of Chinese Islamic education.
As part of the program, it has begun to compile 6 textbooks both

in the Chinese and Uighur languages designed for students of grade one and two: "A Concise Course on Qur'an", "A Concise Course on Hadith", "A Concise Course on Islamic Doctrine", "A Concise Course on Islamic Law", "A Concise Course on World Islamic History", "A Concise Course on Chinese Islamic History". Moreover, it also has been listed in the program to compile "Basic Arabic" (first 4 volumes), "Holy Qur'an Recitation" and "Arabic Calligraphy". Furthermore, the State Religious Affairs Administration is currently organizing a compilation of a 6-category and 10-volume textbook for political education that will be commonly used by all religious colleges and schools. It will help to foster a contingent of religious workers who love both the country and their religion.

5. *Actively Developing Foreign Friendly Contacts*

1). FRIENDLY CONTACTS WITH MUSLIMS IN VARIOUS COUNTRIES AND REGIONS

As the reform and opening up to the outside world progresses further, and the relations with Arab and Islamic countries further develops, the China Islamic Association has built up friendly contacts and cooperation with some Islamic countries in Asia and Africa and also with some international Islamic organizations such as the Muslim World League, the World Islamic Call Society, the Egyptian Islamic Affairs Supreme Council.

Since 1978 when the China Islamic Association received Sheikh Zabara, general Mufti of the Yemeni Republic, for the first time, it has received more than 40 visiting delegations or individuals from many countries and places, and over one thousand foreign guests. Among the visitors some were state leaders or heads of certain Islamic organizations, such as Libyan president Qaddafi, ex-president of Sudan Numeiri, former speaker of the parliament of Iran Rafsanjani, secretary-general of the Muslim World League Dr. Naseef and vice secretary-general Abudi, director of the office of special assistance of the World Islamic Development Bank Dr. Salim, Asia coordinator of the Muslim World League Juma, former secretary-general of the World Muslim Congress Mr. Inamulahan, Saudi Crown Prince Abdul Aziz and Prince Sultan. The Association has also received visiting delegations from Islamic countries or organizations, such as the delegation of the Ministry of Religious Foundation of Morocco, the delegation of the Muslim World League led by Jamjoom (chairman of the Holy Qur'an Committee of MWL and former minister of industry and commerce of Saudi Arabia), president and his companions of the International Islamic University of Pakistan, chief editor and his colleagues of "Pyramids" newspaper from Egypt, the Holy Qur'an reciters from Egypt and Libya, and delegations from Algeria, Somalia, Niger, Brunei, Indonesia, Bangladesh, Malaysia, Iraq, Syria, Hong Kong and Taiwan. What is worth mention is that the secretary-general of the Muslim World League Dr. Naseef went to the Northwest of China to visit Muslim there and was warmly received by the local Muslim community.

The China Islamic Association also dispatched delegations or individuals to attend various international Islamic conferences.

For example, the delegation of the Association attended the 13th Assembly of the Egyptian Islamic Affairs Supreme Council, the 14th International Conference on Islamic Unity in Iran, the 13th Annual Meeting of the World Islamic Call Society in Libya. Imam Chen Guangyuan, president of the Association, visited Hong Kong and Macao at the joint invitation of the Islamic organizations in these two places.

Chinese Muslims have always been concerned about poor Muslims all over the world. The China Islamic Association provided one million RMB in relief for Muslims in Somalia and Afghanistan. In 2002, the Chinese Government provided 100 million US dollars in aid for Afghani refugees.

The Islamic cause in China has received support and help from foreign Muslims as well. The World Islamic Development Bank that has 55 member countries has contributed funds for the construction of Islamic institutes of Xinjiang, Beijing, Ningxia, Kunming, Zhengzhou, Shenyang and Lanzhou, and Tong Arabic School and Tianjin Hui Professional High School. The Muslim World League, the World Islamic Call Society, and the IQRAA Charitable Society have all helped Chinese Muslims with material aid. President of the United Arab Emirates Sheikh Zaid has presented printing equipment to the Association to promote

Islamic culture in China. Saudi Crown Prince Abdul Aziz has also made donations to the Chinese Islamic cause.

In 1987, the China Islamic Association cooperated with the Muslim World League and successfully held the Symposium on Islamic Da'wah, and also cooperated with the Islamic Educational Scientific and Cultural Organization and IQRAA Charitable Society in holding the Experience-Exchanging Class for Arabic Teaching at the China Islamic Institute in 1997.

Over the past 40 years, in response to invitations, the China Islamic Association has sent more than 100 delegations, over

© Chinese Muslim woman at an international conference.

◎ Muslim performing artist Li Jiacun and Muslim calligrapher Wu Siyao draw a picture to commemorate the 1,350th anniversary of the introduction of Islam into China.

300 persons altogether, to take part in various international Islamic conferences, and have been warmly received by government leaders and welcomed by the local Muslims. The friendship and mutual understanding between Muslims of China and the rest of the world has been improved through their visits as a result. The leaders of the Association and Chinese Muslim scholars have also attended activities such as the conference of the Egyptian Islamic Affairs Supreme Council, the conference of the Muslim World League Mosques Supreme Council, the Egyptian Azhar Islamic Da'wah seminar, the conference of the

World Islamic Call Society, the Ramzan Forum of Moroccan King Hassan¢Ú, the Oman International Islamic Law Seminar, the Algerian Islamic Thought Seminar, the International Academic Seminar on Zhenghe in Indonesia, the Mosque Get-Together in celebration of the independence of Indonesia, the Malaysian Islamic Cultural Festival, the Iraq International Arabic Calligraphy and Islamic Decoration Art Festival and the Second Pakistan International Calligraphy and Calligraphic Art Exhibition. Young Chinese Qaris (Qur'an reciters) regularly take part in Qu'ran recitation competitions held in Saudi Arabia, Egypt, Iran and Malaysia.

In line with cultural exchange agreements between China and a number of friendly foreign countries, the Association has sent more than 200 young Chinese Muslim students and in-service Imams to the Islamic institutes of Egypt, Libya and Pakistan for further study or short term training.

The Association has established extensive contacts with many Islamic organizations that enjoy high international reputation, and has developed friendly communications and cooperation with them. For example Ilyas Sheng Xiaxi, consultant to the Association, was a committee member of the Muslim World League Mosque Supreme Council, and was awarded the Star of

Qadi Azem Medal in 1990 by president of Pakistan Ishak Khan; former vice-president and secretary-general of the Association Hanafi Wan Yaobin was a committee member of the Egyptian Islamic Affairs Supreme Council, and former vice-president of the Association Ibrahim Amin and vice secretary-general Yang Zhibo are committee members of the Supreme Council of the World Islamic Call Society.

Besides them, former vice-presidents of the Association Nu'man Ma Xian and Maimaiti Sailai were awarded the Egyptian Presidential First-Grade Special Medal and the Egyptian Presidential Academic Medal respectively by Egyptian President Mubarak. All of these are great honors for all Chinese Muslims.

The China Islamic Association has also developed friendly contacts with Muslims in Hong Kong, Macao and Taiwan, strengthening communication and cooperation with them and working strenuously for the great cause of the reunification of the motherland.

2). RESUMPTION OF PILGRIMAGE

On October 19, 1979, the Chinese Muslim Pilgrim Delegation with Zhang Jie as president went to Mecca for pilgrimage, thus, Chinese Muslims' pilgrimage was resumed after

14 years' suspension. As the living standard keeps improving, more and more Muslims in China travel to Mecca for pilgrimage. It became much more convenient to perform pilgrimage after the Sino-Saudi Arabia diplomatic relationship was established in January of 1990. Statistics show that there are more than 70,000 Chinese Muslims that have performed pilgrimage. The friendly relations between Muslims in China and Arab countries and the rest of the world have been further strengthened through activities such as pilgrimage and visits.

In 1998, the State Religious Affairs Administration held a special meeting on pilgrimage, reiterating to its policy of organized and planned pilgrimage, and placing it in the course of regulated administration.

In 2001, the 200-person Delegation of the Chinese Muslim Pilgrims (King's Guests) led by Yu Zhengui, vice-president and secretary-general of the China Islamic Association, successfully fulfilled the work of pilgrimage. It was the first time that China accepted the invitation of King of Saudi Arabia and organized Chinese Muslims to travel to Mecca for pilgrimage as the King's guests. This has started a new way of organizing pilgrimage delegations for Chinese Muslims.

◎ Leaders of the China Islamic Association see Chinese Hajjis off at the Capital Airport, Beijing.

3). CULTURAL AND ACADEMIC EXCHANGES

There have been frequent contacts and exchanges between the China Islamic Association and the academic circles of Islamic countries in Asia and Africa. The Association has sent many delegations and individuals to take part in various international academic activities, for example in March of 1981, Prof. Na Zhong, consultant to the Association, attended the International Muslim Scholars' Conference held in Islamabad, Pakistan, and delivered a paper titled "The Contributions That Islam Has Made to World Culture". In March of 1983, the Association sent a delegation to participate in the International Islamic Books Exhibition held in the State Museum of Pakistan in Karachi with over a hundred varieties of books and scriptures of the Holy Qur'an, Hadith, Islamic philosophy, Islamic Law, history, Arabic calligraphy and textbooks used in Mosque Education. On December 4-8, 1987, with the help and support of the Association, the Muslim World League successfully held an Islamic seminar in Beijing. It was the first international Islamic meeting held in China since the New China was founded. The participants to the seminar were scholars from Saudi Arabia, Egypt, Pakistan, Sudan, England, Ghana and Turkey, and some Chinese Muslim scholars and the leaders of the China Islamic Association and the Beijing Municipal Islamic Association. Secretary-General of the Muslim World League Dr. Naseef presided over the meeting. The seminar focused on various topics including "Studies on the Traditions of the Prophet", "Holy Qur'an, Hadith, Da'wah Workers' Weapon and Da'wah Method", "Sermon at Juma Prayer and the Da'wah Mission of Mosque" and "Islamic Education and Its Social Effects".

图书在版编目（CIP）数据

中国伊斯兰教／米寿江，尤佳著．—北京：五洲传播出版社，2004.6
（中国宗教基本情况丛书）

ISBN 7-5085-0533-6

Ⅰ．中... Ⅱ．①米...②尤... Ⅲ．伊斯兰教史－中国－英文
Ⅳ．B969.2

中国版本图书馆 CIP 数据核字（2004）第 050776 号

《中国伊斯兰教》

顾　　问：张广林　杨志波

责任编辑：荆孝敏

编辑助理：蔡　程

图片提供：张广林等

设计承制：北京紫航文化艺术有限公司

翻　　译：敏　昶

《中国伊斯兰教》

五洲传播出版社

地址：中国北京北三环中路 31 号　邮编：100088

电话：82008174　网址：www.cicc.org.cn

开本：140 × 210　1/32　印张：7

2004 年 6 月第一版　印数 1-7000

ISBN 7-5085-0533-6／B · 40

定价：48.00元